Speaking
THE
Truth
IN
Love

Christian Mission and Modern Culture

EDITED BY
ALAN NEELY, H. WAYNE PIPKIN,
AND WILBERT R. SHENK

In the series:

Speaking
THE
Truth
IN
Love

New Testament Resources
for a Missional Hermeneutic

JAMES V. BROWNSON

TRINITY PRESS INTERNATIONAL
Harrisburg, Pennsylvania

Trinity Press International, P.O. Box 1321, Harrisburg, PA 17105

Trinity Press International is a division of
the Morehouse Publishing Group.

Cover design: Brian Preuss

Library of Congress Cataloging-in-Publication Data

Brownson, James V.
   Speaking the truth in love : New Testament resources for a
missional hermeneutic / James V. Brownson.
     p.   cm. – (Christian mission and modern culture series)
   Includes bibliographical references.
   ISBN 1-56338-239-3
   1. Missions – Theory – Biblical teaching. 2. Bible. N.T. –
Hermeneutics.   I. Title. II. Series. III. Series: Christian
mission and modern culture.
BV2073.B78 1998
266'.01–dc21   97-32870

Printed in the United States of America

98   99   00   01   02   6   5   4   3   2   1

Contents

Preface to the Series

Both Christian mission and modern culture, widely regarded as antagonists, are in crisis. The emergence of the modern mission movement in the early nineteenth century cannot be understood apart from the rise of technocratic society. Now, at the end of the twentieth century, both modern culture and Christian mission face an uncertain future.

One of the developments integral to modernity was the way the role of religion in culture was redefined. Whereas religion had played an authoritative role in the culture of Christendom, modern culture was highly critical of religion and increasingly secular in its assumptions. A sustained effort was made to banish religion to the backwaters of modern culture.

The decade of the 1980s witnessed further momentous developments on the geopolitical front with the collapse of communism. In the aftermath of the breakup of the system of power blocs that dominated international relations for a generation, it is clear that religion has survived even if its institutionalization has undergone deep change and its future forms are unclear. Secularism continues to oppose religion, while technology has emerged as a major source of power and authority in modern culture. Both confront Christian faith with fundamental questions.

The purpose of this series is to probe these developments from a variety of angles with a view to helping the church understand its missional responsibility to a culture in crisis. One important resource is the church's experience of two centuries of cross-cultural mission that has reshaped the church into a global Christian *ecumene.* The focus of our inquiry will be the church in modern culture. The series (1) examines modern/postmodern culture from a missional point of view; (2) develops the theological agenda that the church in modern culture must address in order to recover its own integrity; and (3) tests fresh conceptualizations of the nature and mission of the church as it engages modern culture. In other words, these volumes are intended to be a forum where conventional assumptions can be challenged and alternative formulations explored.

This series is a project authorized by the Institute of Mennonite Studies, research agency of the Associated Mennonite Biblical Seminary, and supported by a generous grant from the Pew Charitable Trusts.

Editorial Committee

ALAN NEELY
H. WAYNE PIPKIN
WILBERT R. SHENK

1

Missional Interpretation in a Western Context

Hermeneutics, Biblical Theology, and Mission

God creates the church for mission and sends it into the world, across cultural boundaries. There the church bears witness to and participates in God's gracious activity in the world. As the church enters into that mission, it experiences its most demanding and rewarding theological task — the task of interpreting the good news of the gospel in the context of cultural diversity. Every time the gospel moves out into the world and crosses a cultural boundary, Christians must face again a variety of foundational questions: How can the Christian faith be translated into new languages and into new cultural forms? How much of Christian faith is culturally conditioned, and how much is universal? What role should the Bible play in encouraging or in limiting diverse expressions of Christian faith?

These are hermeneutical questions that arise as the church enters into its missional calling. They require us to look carefully at the nature of culture, the character and structure of Christian faith, and the role of Scripture in guiding the church. This book will explore these questions in an attempt to develop a missional hermeneutic, an understanding of the cross-cultural interpretation of Christian faith. The goal is to understand how the church can engage its cross-cultural hermeneutical task in clear and effective ways as it interprets Scripture and lives out Christian faith, in the context of its call to mission.

I come to this problem as a New Testament scholar with interests in hermeneutics and missiology. Over the years, I have discovered that many of the core issues with which I grapple as a New Testament interpreter bear close affinities to the issues that missiologists address as they seek to understand how the gospel moves across cultural boundaries. I have a deepening conviction that the interaction between these two disciplines can be fruitful and mutually enlightening, particularly on hermeneutical issues. This study is an attempt to bring about just such an interaction. Missiologists may wish for much more extensive treatment of contemporary cross-cultural questions. New Testament scholars will quickly detect all the lacunae in the broadly sketched treatments of New Testament texts. However, my purpose is not to be comprehensive in either discipline. Rather, I hope to be suggestive in opening up a new kind of dialogue between missiology and New Testament interpretation that sparks creative perspectives and fresh avenues of exploration.

More specifically, I hope to show in this book how the study of the New Testament can provide tools and perspectives that help to illumine the church's present missiological challenge. The missiological challenge of understanding the gospel across cultural boundaries is essentially a hermeneutical challenge. I find in my study of the New Testament that there are abundant resources there for illumining the hermeneutical challenges that the church faces today as it engages in mission. This book seeks to address the contemporary hermeneutical challenges posed by the church's mission by exploring the way in which the New Testament writers functioned hermeneutically — how they attempted to interpret the gospel as it crossed cultural boundaries in their diverse contexts in the first century.

The method of inquiry we will pursue can be envisioned as two concentric circles. In the inner circle, this study will be focused on how the biblical writers interpreted the gospel in diverse cultural contexts and across cultural lines. Yet that inner circle of interpretation within the canon is encompassed by a larger circle of contemporary missiological interpretation. This larger circle encompasses more than simply the question of how to interpret the Bible. We want to understand not only the Bible in cross-cultural contexts but also the character of Christian faith in its various expressions. We therefore cannot speak in this larger circle only of the interpretation of *texts* as if interpretation were only a cognitive activity focused on reading; we must speak also of interpretation as the complex process by which meaning is created and woven into the whole fabric of our lives. Ultimately, a contemporary missional hermeneutic must illumine not only how texts are read but also how the reading of texts issues in new forms of life. Interpretation in this sense encompasses all the theological activity of the church, especially as the church engages in mission and seeks to find and create meaning in its varied contexts.

The Missional Context of the Church in the West

These hermeneutical issues that arise in the church's mission are exceedingly broad and complex. In every cultural context, they emerge in ways that are distinctive. However, this study proposes to narrow the focus to some extent by looking at the hermeneutical issues that arise in a particular missional context — the context of the church located in Western, First-World culture. This is a context in which the Christian church finds itself in a new and challenging position. For centuries, Western culture has identified itself as "Christendom," as the realm that has come under the sway of the gospel. Yet in the last two or three hundred years, the forces of secularization and modernity have combined to bring about the end of Christendom; we can no longer claim to live in a Christian culture — if we ever did before! (cf. Hauerwas and Willimon 1989).

The end of Christendom places Western Christians in a dramatically new situation. We now recognize that Western culture is not the realm of Christendom that must be brought to the rest of the world as a part of God's mission; rather, the gospel must be addressed in fresh ways to a Western culture that no longer understands or discerns God's gracious activity in the world. Now the hermeneutical challenge consists not in bringing the gospel to some distant and/or "primitive" culture "out there." Rather, the hermeneutical challenge is to bring the gospel to bear upon

Western culture itself, a culture that has become, in many ways, powerfully resistant to Christian faith.

Accordingly, this study seeks to develop a missional hermeneutic not for every time and place, but within a specific context, that of the church in the West. Although much of this study may have relevance in other contexts as well, this study grapples with the hermeneutical questions that are arising for the First-World church as it seeks to read Scripture and to respond to God's call to mission in its new situation. Before turning to hermeneutical issues more specifically, therefore, we must first describe the context in which this study is located, the context that at one time was called "Christendom."

Two realities are apparent to many Christians who reflect upon the present situation of the church's mission in North America and Europe: First, the increasing marginalization in Western culture of religion in general and of the Christian church in particular requires from Christians a fresh vision for what it means to be the Christian church in our post-Christian setting. Second, many Christians also believe that the church's mission is still both viable and urgent. The Christian faith offers good news and hope for our situation, good news that must be lived out and proclaimed with courage and wisdom.

This broad vision is shared by many Christian groups, but it can be further sharpened by discerning more specifically what is happening in our cultural context and what our response should be. First, we must recognize that our current crisis is, in many respects, a legacy from the Enlightenment. Here the writings of Lesslie Newbigin (1986 and 1989) have been especially helpful. Newbigin points out the ways in which the empiricism of the scientific method has pervaded our worldview. This emphasis on the empirical — what can be measured and quantified — has resulted in an unhealthy split between the public and the private realms, between facts and values, between science and religion. Religion in general, and Christian faith in particular, has been relegated to the private realm, where truth claims are immaterial and where disputes are not resolved but simply massaged into docility by psychological and sociological analysis. As a result, the public sphere is increasingly stripped of any moral framework (those are private issues), and society as a whole more and more resembles some giant machine gone amok, driven by rapidly expanding economic and technological powers but devoid of any sense of purpose or even a clear sense of the common good.

Second, we must also recognize another powerful cultural force affecting our situation — the dynamics of postmodernism. Whereas Enlightenment thinkers hoped for a grand synthesis of all human arts and cultures under the banner of reason and science, a postmodern perspective consciously and explicitly eschews such a goal. Postmodernism recognizes that even reason and science cannot always be relied upon to resolve disputes and settle truth claims. Rather, reason and science are often merely tools in the hands of deeper and more powerful forces such as economic and class conflicts, ethnic and racial hostilities, gender divisions and the like. The title of Alasdair MacIntyre's recent book underscores the problem: *Whose Justice? Which Rationality?* (1988). The postmodern world is a world in which pluralism constantly threatens to devolve into factionalism, in which anomie becomes a perpetual existential reality, and in which the resolution of disputes becomes increasingly problematic, frequently disintegrating into a clutching after power and its dark counterpart, the proliferation of violence.

The challenge of postmodernism moves the discussion regarding the church's mission to a much deeper level. The question is no longer simply how Christian faith can reenter the public sphere; the public sphere itself has been fractured into a variety of competing interest groups. Now the questions revolve much more around issues of identity, lifestyle, and political strategy: How are Christians to live and bear witness in such a chaotic situation? How can the gospel's claim that Jesus is the gracious Savior and therefore Lord of the cosmos become intelligible in a context where such claims are suspiciously regarded as yet another bid for power from yet another interest group? Whereas the Enlightenment threatened to turn all religious truth claims into matters of private opinion and feeling, postmodernism threatens to turn the Christian message of mercy and peace into a mask concealing a political grab for domination and control.

Such is the context in which Western Christians are called to read and interpret the Scripture. Such is the context that they are called to interpret in light of the Scripture. It is a context that calls us to reconsider, at perhaps a deeper level than before, what it means to "speak the truth in love" (Eph. 4:15). What does it mean to be called to speak of the gospel as *truth* in a culture that declares that religious speech can never be true, but only "true-for-you"? How can we speak and enact the truth from a posture of loving servanthood in a culture that interprets truth claims as political strategies masking inevitable self-interests? And finally, what is the role of Scripture in leading us to the truth and in teaching us how to speak it?

The Problem of Diversity in Biblical Interpretation

With these questions from the Western cultural context in mind, we turn more specifically to the challenge of finding resources from Scripture to illumine the church's present missiological challenge. As soon as we begin to look to the Scripture for light on these questions, however, we confront the problems we have just described in a new way. The fragmentation of postmodernism is nearly as pervasive within various sectors of the church as it is beyond it. We may even agree with other Christians that the Bible is our final witness to truth, yet we often find ourselves disagreeing with each other, often radically, over precisely what that truth is and how it should be understood. Hence it is not enough merely to look to the Bible for answers. We must look to the Bible, to be sure, but we must also examine *how* we look to the Bible.

Two issues are at stake here. One concerns diverse expressions of Christian faith that are found in the canon of Scripture itself; the other concerns diverse ways of reading and interpreting Scripture, and expressing Christian faith today. These two issues are deeply intertwined. This section will address the latter of these issues — the problem of diverse ways of reading Scripture and expressing Christian faith today. In the next two chapters, we will turn to the former problem of the diversities within Scripture itself.

We need a model for contemporary biblical interpretation that is able to address the problems and challenges of plurality in interpretation. We need not only to observe various differences in interpretation; we need also to have some understanding of how to evaluate them. We must ask: When are differences in interpretation a sign of healthy diversity, and when are they a signal that some people are simply mistaken or deficient in the way that they read the Bible? Is the Bible a kind of Rorschach blot in which interpreters will necessarily find whatever it is that they are looking for? Or are there controls, disciplines, and parameters that help to mediate between contrasting or conflicting interpretations? These are hotly debated issues in current hermeneutical discussions, and we need a model for interpretation that will help us address these questions.

For some, diversity in biblical interpretation is merely the sign of an unfinished task. If we cannot agree on what the Bible is saying to our world, we need to keep talking and reading with greater effort and intensity until we do agree. Yet such an approach has often led to one of two unfortunate results. Either Christians have become totally absorbed in endlessly — and often unproductively — attempting to reconcile their differences (e.g., certain sectors of the ecumenical movement), or they have continually separated themselves from other Christians who are deemed as heretical or lapsed (e.g., evangelical Protestantism). These twin failures of the Western churches betray a common inability to deal constructively with diversity in interpretation.

But the problem of diversity in interpretation runs

deeper than mere interpretive disagreements and the mechanisms for their resolution. At a deeper level, the challenge of postmodernism creates an increasing absence of any universal frame of reference. We find it harder to keep our bearings and to connect with each other. The postmodern emphasis on the contingent, the particular, and the subjective makes it difficult to find bases for dialogue, common ground where diverse groups may gather and fruitfully interact with each other. Even within the church, it is becoming evident to us that there is no fixed point, free from presuppositions and biases, from which any of us may interpret the Bible. We all begin from some sort of model, some integrated framework of understanding about the nature of religion, the character of our social and cultural context, the status of the text, and so forth. Bultmann referred to such models as our "preunderstanding" (*Vorverständnis*). Gadamer and Thiselton refer to a "horizon" of expectation. David Kelsey uses the notion of a *discrimen* to refer to such a model. Our differing horizons sometimes make it difficult for us to understand the way that others read Scripture and even to talk with others about our diverse understandings of the biblical texts. Whatever the particular terminology we may use, we need to learn to identify what our hermeneutical models are and how they work for us in our context.

Thus any biblical hermeneutic is not merely pretheological, laying out the ground rules for reading Scripture before theological reflection begins. Rather, a biblical hermeneutic that is honest and self-critical must necessarily be *theological* in character. The very image of "horizon" implies a *cosmos,* a world that is in view. That world in turn implies a *cosmology*, a comprehensive and synthetic perspective that makes understanding possible at all and that enables meaning to take shape. If we are to speak meaningfully to our complex situation and if we are to understand the diversities that characterize Christian witness itself, we need to discuss the meaning and function of our horizons. We must lay out our preunderstanding of the nature and character of God, of God's relationship with the world, and of our essential humanness. That horizon of expectation is always subject to revision, movement, and widening. Yet we must acknowledge and subject to critical examination our assumptions and presuppositions in interpretation. Otherwise we will be able neither to understand the points at which we differ from others in our interpretation of the Bible nor to speak meaningfully in our world.

Conclusion

This chapter has ranged rather widely, addressing the way in which hermeneutics grows out of mission, the dynamics of the church in Western culture, and the problems of plurality in the interpretation of Scripture. Yet it is the thesis of this book that these three issues need to be addressed in concert with each other. The hermeneutics of biblical interpretation and of missional proclamation are intimately related and intertwined. The new missional context of the church in relation to Western culture brings the church back to its Scripture in search of wisdom to illumine its new situation. Yet in many ways, the church's encounter with Scripture seems to reflect the same struggles that the church experiences in relating to its Western context. The following chapters will explore how a closer look at the biblical materials may help to open a fresh way through this impasse and enable us to speak the truth in love in our Western context.

2

A Hermeneutic of Diversity

Introduction

In this chapter, I begin to sketch out a model for interpreting both Scripture and Christian faith that takes seriously both the data of the biblical text and the nature of our contemporary context. I want to develop a model that faces honestly the reality of pluralism and diversity in our modern and postmodern setting. I will argue that at many points we read the Bible differently from one another and express our faith differently, not because one person is wrong and another right, but because we come from different contexts. This argument, if correct, leads to a second basic question: How can we approach the interpretation of the Bible and of Christian faith in general so as to allow for a plurality of expressions of faith, while at the same time allowing the biblical text to exercise a controlling and shaping influence on each particular expression? How can we acknowledge our own particularity and that of others — and the limits that those particularities entail — and yet seek to speak the truth not just for ourselves but to others as well?

This question ultimately leads us back to the issue of

"speaking the truth in love." Some may be so preoccupied with defending the truth of the Bible that they are threatened by diversity in interpretation, which seems to engulf the Bible in the postmodern crisis that threatens the stability of all knowledge. Others may be so concerned for love and tolerance that they are reluctant to speak of the Bible's witness to truth at all, thereby reducing the Bible's witness to matters of personal preference and opinion. Between such a Scylla and Charybdis there seems to be no safe passage. Yet I believe that a closer attention to the biblical texts themselves can provide us with resources for addressing these dilemmas. In what follows, therefore, I will explore how the Bible itself addresses the question of the coherence of truth and challenge of cultural plurality.

Some Presuppositions

I call the hermeneutical model I am developing a *missional* hermeneutic because it springs from a basic observation about the New Testament: The early Christian movement that produced and canonized the New Testament was a movement with a specifically *missionary* character. One of the most obvious phenomena of early Christianity is the way in which the movement crossed cultural boundaries and planted itself in new places. Most of the New Testament was in fact written by people engaged in and celebrating this sort of missionary enterprise in the early church. This tendency of early Christianity to cross cultural boundaries is a fertile starting point for developing a model of interpretation. It is fertile, especially for our purposes, because it places the question of the expression of Christianity in diverse cultures at the top of the interpretative agenda. This focus may be of great help to us in grappling with plurality in interpretation today.

Yet before we explore such a missional hermeneutic biblically, I must first make clear some of my own assumptions that will shape the way I approach interpretative issues. I will attempt in this chapter to provide arguments and evidence to support these assumptions, but it will be helpful first to see where the argument as a whole is going. The missional hermeneutic I am advocating begins by affirming the reality and inevitability of plurality in interpretation. Because every reading of the Bible is shaped by the individuality and the historical and cultural particularity of the interpreter, there will always be multiple interpretations of the Bible. Therefore plurality in interpretation is not necessarily a sign of interpretative failure, but often of interpretative effectiveness, reflecting a distinctive convergence of the text with the particular context of the reader.

Such an affirmation of interpretative diversity is not without its critics. Some argue that the intention of the author must curb diversity in interpretation. We must interpret the texts as their original writers intended them to be interpreted, and in no other way. I agree that texts should not be interpreted in ways that violate their author's intention. Yet authorial intention is often very difficult to determine with precision. Authors sometimes write with multiple or obscure intentions, or with intentions that are not fully formed or that are conflicting. Even when the author's intention can be discerned, there often remains room for multiple interpretations at many points within the author's stated overall intention. There is always what Paul Ricoeur calls a "surplus of meaning."

Others may argue that the plain sense of the text must be a curb on diversity in interpretation. Again, I agree that interpretations should not violate the original lexical-grammatical sense of a text. Yet most of the more interesting and important texts in the Bible have meanings that extend well beyond the "plain sense" of the text. What is the plain sense of the sentence "I am the way, the truth and the life"? At one level, of course, the answer is simple, but if we want to press further to determine what the sentence means in its fullness, we need to inquire into the metaphorical, rhetorical, and symbolic dimensions of language and not merely its plain sense.

But there is an even more important reason why diversity in interpretation is to be regarded as necessary and appropriate, and not always as a sign of interpretative failure. Every interpretation is an attempt to convey meaning within and to a specific context. Interpretation is always social, contextual, and relational. Although the author's encoded meaning in a text may remain stable and even perhaps relatively accessible, what an interpreter finds meaningful in that text may change dramatically from one context to another. Christians often speak of finding new discoveries in every fresh reading of the Bible. Hence diversity in interpretation cannot and should not always be avoided.

At the same time, any thoughtful hermeneutic must also affirm the value of dialogue with other readers of the biblical text. Every time we read a commentary, every time we hear someone else talk about a passage, we discover new perspectives that we had not seen before. Dialogue in interpretation often results in the correction of idiosyncratic or distorted readings of Scripture within any given context. Therefore there is also a sense in which plurality in interpretation is not always a sign of interpretative effectiveness, but sometimes a result of defective or inadequate readings that may be corrected or qualified through dialogue with other interpreters.

How can plurality in interpretation be at one point a sign of interpretative success and at another point a sign of deficiency? The answer lies in the multifaceted nature of interpretation itself. Every interpretative reading is an attempt to project a symbolic world in which the world of the text and the world of the reader are brought together in such a way that each mutually informs the other. Where there is a diversity of readers, there will always be a plurality of interpretations; each reader brings his or her own distinctive "world" into a conversation with the text. But these "worlds" in which text and context are brought together are not totally dissimilar. Every interpretation must do justice to the same text. Moreover, every interpretation must connect, in some way, with our basic humanity. To be meaningful, every interpretation must address in some way the common "stuff" of all our lives — the wider forms of rationality that we share as well as our shared experiences of birth, death, contingency, relatedness, anxiety, love, loss, and the like. Diversity in interpretation is healthy when it emerges from our human diversity; diversity in interpretation is deficient when it distorts our common text or fails to connect with our common humanity.

However, our discussion of common humanity raises the

need both for a cautionary note and for a clarification. First the cautionary note: The meaning of our common humanity and its relationship to our own particularity is not entirely established prior to the act of interpretation. There are of course certain innate features of human life, evident cross-culturally, that characterize us as a species. Yet such characteristics offer only a minimal portrait of what it means to be human. The full dimensions of our common humanity are discovered only in the process of dialogical interpretation with others, as we discover what we share. A missional hermeneutic calls diverse interpreters to read a common text with a commitment to be faithful both to the world of the text and to their own shared and distinctive worlds. When this takes place, the contours and character-istics of both the unity and the diversity of human life are more clearly disclosed.

The clarification regarding our common humanity con-cerns the relationship between that common humanity and the Bible. Implicit in my discussion to this point is the assumption that the Bible itself offers a distinctive vision of what it means to be truly human. Such a vision is not immediately accessible on the surface of the biblical text, and interpreters may often confuse culturally specific di-mensions of the biblical narrative with a more universal vision of our common humanity. Despite these difficulties, however, this study proceeds on the assumption that the Bible has something to say to all of us, regardless of our cultural diversity, about what it means to be human. Al-though we will rarely discover all that the Bible has to say on this subject apart from intercultural dialogue and reflec-tion, a missional hermeneutic assumes that cross-cultural dialogue surrounding the interpretation of Scripture offers distinctive opportunities for the discernment of our common humanity — opportunities that may not be as significantly present in the reading of just any other text.

Biblical Grounding of a Missional Hermeneutic

This dialectic between our common humanity and our cultural particularity — a dialectic that lies at the heart of a missional hermeneutic — is itself reflected in the narratives of Scripture. These narratives reflect the basic missional structure of Christian faith. God calls and blesses people in all their particularity, but always with a view to the wider humanity that is the object of God's gracious concern. Already in the story of the call of Abraham, the divine call and blessing come to a particular person in a specific cultural context. Yet from the beginning, the texts set the story within a universal context:

> "I will make of you a great nation, and I will bless you, and make your name great, so that you will be a blessing. I will bless those who bless you, and the one who curses you I will curse; and in you all the families of the earth shall be blessed" (Gen. 12:2–3).

In Abraham, the particularity of God's blessing also moves out to "all the families of the earth."

Later in the monarchical and second temple period, this convergence of a particular calling and a universal context gave rise to dreams of the hegemony of a beneficent Israelite sovereignty. Isaiah 2:2–4 puts the vision in these words:

In days to come
>   the mountain of the LORD's house
shall be established as the highest of the mountains,
>   and shall be raised above the hills;
all the nations shall stream to it.
>   Many peoples shall come and say,
"Come, let us go up to the mountain of the LORD,
>   to the house of the God of Jacob;
that he may teach us his ways
>   and that we may walk in his paths."
For out of Zion shall go forth instruction,
>   and the word of the LORD from Jerusalem.
He shall judge between the nations,
>   and shall arbitrate for many peoples;
they shall beat their swords into plowshares,
>   and their spears into pruning hooks;
nation shall not lift up sword against nation,
>   neither shall they learn war any more.

Again, the particularity of Israel's call moves out toward a universal salvific purpose.

We find the same dialectic in the Gospels. On the one hand, Jesus is consistently portrayed in all four Gospels as one who enacts a highly focused and culturally particularistic vocation: "I was sent only to the lost sheep of the house of Israel" (Matt. 15:24). At the same time, however, the Gospels portray Jesus in such a way that this particularity is always "stretched" and placed in a larger context. Jesus reaches out to the outcasts and the unclean. He uses a Samaritan as the hero of a parable. Most of all, he announces the coming reign of God, with overwhelming implications not only for Israel but for the whole world. Judgment and salvation are coming to the house of Israel, but that is only the beginning. The whole earth will be summoned to stand before the judgment seat.

A decisive turn takes place, however, in the story of the emergence of the church as recorded in the Acts of the Apostles and the New Testament epistles. When Gentiles are incorporated into the people of God *as Gentiles,* the interaction between particularity and universality is completely recast. No longer is God's universal saving purpose spoken of as the beneficent hegemony of Israelite culture and power; rather, God's universal saving purpose is disclosed in the sanctifying of many different political and cultural contexts, both Jewish and Gentile. Gentiles need not become Jews, and Jews need not become Gentiles. Each in their own context and culture glorifies the one God who is Lord of all. Revelation 5:9 celebrates the work of the Lamb who "ransomed for God saints from every tribe and language and people and nation." Every ethnicity, every language, every political context, every different social grouping becomes a potential source of doxology and praise to God. The particularity of each setting is placed in a universal context, not by dreams of hegemony, but by the apprehension of a particular saving story that discloses a God who seeks to be glorified by a diversity of languages, ethnicities, and peoples. In the New Testament, the flow of blessing is reversed. No longer do the nations stream to Jerusalem; the word of the Lord goes out to the ends of the earth. All of humanity is called to glorify God, not by suppressing diversity and particularity, but by sanctifying it. The universal bond of humanity appears not so much in its set of common responses to its creator and sustainer, but rather by humanity's diverse responses to the particular vision of God disclosed in the story of the life, death, and resurrection of Jesus Christ.

Theological Implications
of a Missional Hermeneutic

When the overall message of Scripture is interpreted in this manner, the result is a distinctive rendering of the identity of God. In his book *The Uses of Scripture in Recent Theology*, David Kelsey has observed that the way we bring Scripture to bear in the making of theological proposals is directly connected to our understanding of "the mode in which God is present among the faithful" (1975:160ff.). Kelsey argues that at the center of every theological proposal is a *discrimen*, "an imaginative construal of the mode of God's presence *pro nobis* that tries to catch up all its complexity and utter singularity in a single metaphorical judgment" (:161). This *discrimen* is not so much a norm that governs each theological proposal as it is a criterion that enables various theological utterances to find their place with respect to the theological structure as a whole. It captures in relatively brief compass a characteristic vision and understanding of the way in which God's presence and saving activity manifests itself. Our attempt to ground a missional hermeneutic in this particular reading of the Bible implies a certain *discrimen* that characterizes our approach. To put it simply, a missional hermeneutic begins with the assumption that the mode in which God is present among the faithful is irreducibly *multicultural*. The reality of God's presence is at least potentially available within the symbolic world projected by any specific culture. Although each culture is called to repentance, its specific contours are not obliterated. Hence in early Christianity, the sacred books were translated into other languages; church organization followed the patterns of other clubs and civic groups; the categories of Hellenistic philosophy were used to articulate the meaning of the gospel in that context (cf. Sanneh 1989). Yet at the same time, a missional hermeneutic includes the awareness that the reality of God is not exhausted by any particular culture's ways of naming and worshiping God.

It is this awareness, I would argue, that explains the dynamism of the early church in its mission. There appears to be a powerful drive throughout much of the New Testament to move the Christian gospel across cultural lines and into new contexts. On the one hand, this drive emerges from a perception of God's mercy and grace that extends to all. In this sense, the cross-cultural proclamation of the gospel is an expression of the universal salvific purpose of God. On the other hand, however, the urge to bring the Christian gospel across diverse cultural boundaries has a *doxological* origin as well. In Romans 15:9ff., Paul says that the whole reason for the mission to the Gentiles was "that the Gentiles might glorify God for his mercy." God is more greatly glorified when praise comes from diverse peoples and diverse cultures.

The *discrimen* discussed above entails two further assumptions: that each culture's apprehension of God in Scripture may be accurate but is always provisional, and that God is most fully known and glorified through a diversity of cultures and cultural perspectives. These two assumptions provide the theological context for grappling with the whole question of the creativity and particularity of the reader. A missional hermeneutic presupposes one God, one Scripture, and one sacred story. At the same time, however, this sacred story does not serve to promote or sanction a monocultural religious perspective but rather a multicultural one. God's presence is irreducibly multicultural. This affirmation serves to sanction a distinctive and particular dimension in each reading of Scripture. At the same time, it challenges these particular readings to enter into a creative dialogue with other readings of the text. The goal is not to suppress the distinctive characteristics of each reading. Rather, the purpose is to enrich and to deepen the disclosure of God's glory through an awareness of the diverse ways in which God is moving through the world in mercy, eliciting doxology in many cultures. Diverse readings of the Bible find a point of coherence, not in some "standard" or universally accepted way of reading the Bible and expressing Christian faith, but in the awareness that the God whose presence calls forth a distinctive form of doxology in one culture is the same God whose mercy calls forth grateful praise as well from other cultures, in other forms.

A missional hermeneutic therefore underscores a specific understanding of the experience of salvation. Its assumption is that God's saving power comes to each culture in both affirmation and critique. In Acts 17 Paul quotes Greek philosophers and also calls his hearers to repentance. Despite its initial word of judgment and call to repentance, the experience of salvation as described in the New Testament is, finally, in some sense the experience of "coming home," of fulfilling one's destiny, of finding one's rightful

3

meneutic of Coherence

pter argued for a hermeneutical posture
ality in the interpretation of Christian
ity is not only hermeneutically necessary
pression of fundamental claims made by
ng the identity and purpose of God. Our
this point has focused primarily on what
k the truth *in love*, aware of and respect-
ces, longing for the emergence of a full
diversity. However, such a posture, by it-
lissolve into an infinite number of diverse
adings of the Bible and an equal number
ressions of Christian faith. In order for a
etation to be healthy, the centrifugal ten-
versity and particularity must be balanced
ces that also move toward consensus and

reasons why this centripetal tendency
ed. First, all biblical interpreters are wres-
ne texts. There already is a commonality
cal interpreters commit themselves in one

place in the cosmos. The New Testament makes it clear,
however, that salvation takes diverse forms within the lives
of specific Christian communities. Those diverse forms are
directly related to the different cultural and social settings
in which the gospel takes root. In one context, forgiveness
of sins may be the central focus; in another, reconciliation to
God and to others; in yet another, the reception of the Holy
Spirit or the receiving of divine life in the here and now.
The divine blessing assumes shape and form only within
specific contexts and always in diverse ways. Each culture
is called to repentance; yet a missional hermeneutic understands that call to repentance not as the obliteration of each
culture but rather as the *sanctification* of each cultural setting so that it may offer a fuller and more perfect praise
to God. Repentance is not an abandoning of identity but a
turning toward God.

However, the Christian experience of salvation is not
only a matter of experiencing the purification and sanctification of one's own cultural and social setting. It also
involves a heightened sense of connectedness to other diverse cultural settings where praise is also given to God.
The Christian experience of salvation not only purifies and
enriches one's distinctive cultural identity. It also deepens
the awareness that one participates with all of humanity in
a multicultural worship of God that transcends any particular context. Hence the Christian experience of salvation
creates a dual identity: on the one hand, I am a member
of a particular community that offers its own distinctive
praise to God; and, on the other hand, I am a member of a
diverse human community that offers a much more powerful, indeed astonishing, array of voices, singing a form of

doxology that radically transcends my own distinctive voice. That is why Paul in his letters is able to offer very focused and specific pastoral advice tailored to each setting and at the same time affirm that "our citizenship is in heaven" (Phil. 3:20).

The dynamism of a missional hermeneutic is found precisely in the interplay between these two sources of Christian identity. It entails a vision of a gracious God who enters deeply into the everyday particularity of each cultural setting, each society, each family, each meal, each social interaction. And at the same time, this God invites us to widen our vision to a vast human community of which we are a small part. We are invited to sing our particular melody line in a vast polyphony that so dramatically transcends our own voice that we may wonder if it is ever heard. Yet this vision of God insists that each voice is always heard, that each voice has infinite value, and that there is no song unless each single voice sings, each in its own distinctive way.

Conclusion

This chapter has attempted to bring together two different lines of argumentation. The first line is a hermeneutical argument about diversity in interpretation. From a hermeneutical perspective, diversity in interpretation is necessary and unavoidable, even though there may be limits on such appropriate diversity. The dynamics of reading and interpretation make such diversity necessary. The second line of argument is a theological one. Here we have argued that there is a powerful line of development within the

canon of Scri
expressions of
coherence surr
the character a

These twin
aries of what w
interpretation o
ties for what it r
welcoming diver
that widening o
a loss of any ser
and of Christian
must address in

The previous
that affirms
faith. This pl
but is also an
the Bible rega
discussion up
it means to s
ful of diverse
humanity, ric
self, could eas
and conflictin
of conflicting
model for int
dencies towar
by centripeta
coherence.

There are
must be reco
tling with th
to which all

way or another. Because we are reading the same Bible, we cannot ignore the ways that others read it. Second, all interpreters share a common humanity. Although our experiences may be very diverse, we recognize common experiences that bind us to other human beings as well. Insofar as we are attempting to make the Bible and Christian faith in general meaningful to us today, we also are attempting to make it meaningful to others who share our common humanity.

These two realities — our common text and our common humanity — require that we not only affirm diversity in interpretation, but also that we seek for coherence and commonality in the ways that we interpret Scripture and Christian faith in general. When we turn to the New Testament, however, our quest for coherence and for commonality encounters a difficult challenge: Not only are specific New Testament passages interpreted differently by different people, but within the New Testament as a whole there appears to be a great deal of diversity. New Testament scholars have long recognized that there is a diversity of theological perspectives, contexts, and concerns expressed by the various New Testament books. The trend of most New Testament scholarship in the last two hundred years has been to highlight these contrasts in perspective.

This awareness of the diversity within the New Testament canon is both helpful and problematic. It is helpful because it underscores the thesis we have already advanced, that plurality in religious experience and perspective is to be regarded as normal within the context of early Christianity. It is problematic, however, because the diversity in the New Testament books calls into question whether the

New Testament is capable of functioning as a truly common text. If there is no center to the New Testament, but only a set of competing religious perspectives that do not cohere, then the quest for coherence in contemporary biblical interpretation is a vain one. There can be no coherence in interpretation if the texts themselves do not cohere.

The present discussion addresses the problem of the coherence or center of the New Testament. I want to begin by looking, not at the individual New Testament documents, but at the New Testament as a whole. The very fact that twenty-seven early Christian documents are gathered into a single book called the New Testament entails a particular set of assumptions of which the interpreter must become aware. At the very least, the collection of these various documents into the New Testament canon involves the ascription of some sort of wholeness or coherence to the collection of books. Correspondingly, if one wants to identify oneself as an interpreter of the New Testament, one of the tasks involved is the attempt to grasp and to articulate the way in which a reading of the New Testament *as a whole* can convey meaning.

Of course, one may certainly engage in the interpretation of particular New Testament documents without recognizing or attributing any "wholeness" to the New Testament canon in its entirety. However, it is usually the case that people who identify themselves as religious interpreters of the New Testament are engaged in the pursuit of meaning, not only in particular fragments or books of the New Testament, but in the New Testament as a whole, and it is precisely this kind of pursuit that this chapter examines. Perhaps of even more importance, our ability to move toward convergence and consensus with other interpreters on the meaning of Christian faith as a whole will be directly related to the extent to which we are able to articulate a sense of the coherence of the New Testament as a whole.

What Is "the Gospel"?

In my judgment, one of the most helpful ways to grapple with the question of the coherence of the New Testament is to raise the question, What is "the gospel"? In all three Synoptic Gospels, Jesus is portrayed as one who proclaims the gospel (Matt. 4:23, 9:35; Mark. 1:14; Luke 4:18, 43, etc.). Paul identifies himself as one "set apart for the gospel of God" (Rom. 1:1) and regards the gospel as "the power of God for salvation to everyone who has faith" (Rom. 1:16). A quick glance at a concordance shows that these examples could be multiplied many times. Clearly the term gospel is a kind of code word for many New Testament writers that summarizes something very basic regarding what early Christians thought Christian faith to be all about.

Yet it is not at all easy to press further and to specify exactly *what* the gospel is. The problem is twofold. First, there is an exegetical problem. Although the use of the term gospel in the New Testament suggests some coherent center from which New Testament faith springs, we have already noted how the last two centuries of New Testament scholarship have brought to light the wide-ranging diversity that exists within the New Testament canon. From a purely exegetical point of view, the various theological expressions in the New Testament threaten to become so diverse and disparate that no overarching unity may be found. We have grown accustomed to recognizing the contrasts between the theology of Luke and Paul, or between Mark and Hebrews, for example. But on the whole, scholars in the last two centuries have found it easier to note the contrasts than to find the points of convergence.[1]

The second problem in defining the gospel arises in the hermeneutical arena. New Testament scholars who try to explore the center, or heart, of Christian faith have proposed a variety of models for conceptualizing and articulating that sought-for center, using terms and categories that are intended to be viable and meaningful to people today. These different models are often based on very different presuppositions about what New Testament theology or Christian faith *is* in the first place. Is Christian faith primarily a set of theological axioms? A moral posture? A way of understanding and defining one's own self? A response to God's "mighty acts"? A way of building and maintaining human communities? The way we answer such questions will determine the models we use to construe the "center" of the New Testament, and consequently, the way we think about the meaning and function of the term gospel. Even if one attempts to arrive at an understanding of Christian faith that embraces many of these categories in some overarching system, there will inevitably be characteristic emphases which emerge that will differ from person to person and from place to place. Indeed, the very attempt to define gospel in such a systematic fashion is itself laden with presuppositions about the nature of the term "gospel."

Therefore, any attempt to articulate the essence or coherence of the gospel encounters problems arising from two different kinds of pluralism: (1) the diverse expressions of Christian life and faith within the New Testament and (2) the diverse models for understanding Christian faith and life that are presupposed by various contemporary interpreters.

How is one to find a center in the midst of such diversity? From an exegetical point of view, one must look through the New Testament documents for recurring motifs and themes, common structures, patterns of narrative, lines of development, "trajectories," and the like. Such strategies may assist in finding commonality amidst the pluralities of the New Testament. Yet this *exegetical* quest for the coherence of the New Testament must be accompanied by a *hermeneutical* self-criticism in which interpreters evaluate their way of conceptualizing Christian faith and life in light of the whole range of exegetical data, the plurality of articulations of Christian faith in the past and in the world today. The overall models we use to understand and articulate the essence of New Testament faith must be established and confirmed by exegetical exploration and broadened by exposure to other interpretative approaches and assumptions.

In this dialectic between exegesis and hermeneutics, there are two natural tendencies to be guarded against. The discipline of exegesis naturally tends toward atomism in laying out the data in all its particularity and diversity; hermeneutical considerations are naturally inclined to be reductionistic. The desire for coherence and meaning can result in the suppression of data that do not fit one's own mold. These tensions can be neither escaped nor fully resolved. Each approach must simply restrain the excesses of the other. The quality of one's interpretative work will depend upon the degree to which these tensions are made explicitly the object of reflection and criticism. Hence it is important to acknowledge the preliminary interpretative assumptions that both launch and guide our investigation of the coherence of the New Testament. My purpose in so doing is not to grant these assumptions a privileged or a priori status; quite the opposite. It is to present these assumptions as an initial hypothesis to be attested or corrected by ensuing exegetical and hermeneutical exploration.

Some Assumptions

First, I attempt to articulate the coherence of Christian faith as it finds expression within the bounds of the New Testament canon. By restricting itself to these documents, this study tries to make more explicit the nature of the Christian church's claim that the New Testament canon bears witness to "one holy catholic and apostolic faith." In a sense, this discussion is an attempt to determine the exegetical and hermeneutical basis for the church's use of the canon of the New Testament as the "rule of faith." Is there a coherence or center to be discovered in the New Testament, in the midst of the many theological and situational pluralities found there?

Second, this discussion seeks to avoid two hermeneutical extremes: On the one hand, we must avoid a hermeneutical imperialism that insists on only one possible interpretation of biblical texts and their center. On the other hand, we must also be wary of a deconstructionist nihilism that regards the biblical text as infinitely elastic and subject to an innumerable variety of conflicting interpretations, all of which have an equal claim to legitimacy. We will seek for a genuine coherence in the New Testament that allows for and invites a plurality of interpretations but recognizes certain constraints, implicit in the text, that may set limits on the range of possible interpretations of the gospel.

In this effort to generate a constructive proposal, it may be useful to identify some basic questions that prompt the search for "the gospel" questions that should guide the way in which it is articulated:

1. What is the unity amidst the diversity of the New Testament by which the canon was formed and by which the early Christian movement can be termed a coherent entity?

2. Compared with its Jewish origins, early Christianity represents a religious movement that struck out in some surprisingly new directions. This raises the question: What are the criteria by which early Christians, on the one hand, exercised such astonishing freedom with respect to their earlier Jewish tradition and, on the other hand, preserved so much of that tradition?

3. Similarly, the early Christian movement that produced the New Testament was itself a dynamic and developing phenomenon. How and why did it develop in the way that it did? What criteria did New Testament writers use when they selected and adapted the Christian tradition that they received? For example, by what hermeneutical logic do Matthew and Luke at some points draw on and repeat Mark, and yet at other points exercise a surprising freedom in rewriting the tradition as it is expressed in Mark? The problem appears with even greater sharpness when the Fourth Gospel is compared to the synoptic tradi-

tion, although in this case the lines of dependency are more difficult to ascertain.

4. Our study has already shown how early Christianity manifested itself as a religious perspective that was extraordinarily adaptable to a variety of specific situations. At some points, this adaptability appears to be so pervasive that the points of divergence among different New Testament expressions of Christian faith almost seem more extensive than their points of convergence. What is the key to this adaptability, by what logic or pattern does it operate, and what are its limits?

It should be noted that in each of these questions, the diversity and dynamic character of the New Testament is affirmed; the challenge is to discover the implicit logic and assumptions that both drive and constrain that dynamism and diversity. If we can identify and render explicit that logic and those assumptions, we may be able to articulate a vision for the coherence of the New Testament that invites a variety of creative readings of the New Testament within a dynamic but coherent framework. In other words, if we can discover how the New Testament unites its creative and divergent expressions of faith, we too may discover how to engage in a genuinely dialogical act of interpretation that neither merely echoes the words of the New Testament, nor imposes an alien perspective on the New Testament documents.

The Character of New Testament Documents

It will be useful to begin our quest for this paradigm by which to construe the gospel by talking about the New

Testament itself. Any paradigm that seeks to provide an integrated understanding of these documents must grapple with the characteristic features necessary to describe them. One of the most important of these is the specific historical situation from which these documents emerged and to which they were directed. The specific situation, culture, and worldview of each writer and original reader/hearer affected to a significant degree the way the biblical writers expressed themselves. Although Paul uses the same letter genre in both Galatians and Romans, for example, he writes very differently in the two documents because these two congregations have very different relationships with Paul and are facing different issues in different historical and cultural settings. The consideration of historical context includes not only the attempt to make judgments regarding the historicity of particular events alleged in the texts but, of more importance, the attempt to reconstruct the cultural, religious, political, socioeconomic, and environmental context in which these documents originated. In the last two hundred years, the consideration of the historical context of New Testament texts has made enormous strides, and scholars now have a wealth of data at their disposal that can help to illumine the particular shape, form, and focus of the various New Testament documents, in light of their historical context.

However, a consideration of historical or contextual elements is not sufficient in itself to provide an adequate description of the New Testament documents. The reason is that the biblical texts are more than mere *ad hoc* responses to specific historical situations and contexts. In some way or another, these documents seek to bring a religious *tra-*

dition to bear upon their situations. That religious tradition
has two basic components: the Hebrew Bible or Septuagint
(and other literature reflecting on these texts) on the one
hand, and stories about Jesus, Christian hymns, and other
Christian traditional material on the other. Both the Jewish
and Christian traditions are also shaped by influences from
other cultural, religious, and philosophical traditions as well.

In essence, then, the New Testament might be understood as the attempt of certain writers to address their
specific situations in light of prior Jewish and Christian
traditions. Hence the various New Testament documents
must be evaluated both *at the level of tradition* — because
they draw different elements from the same tradition or
from different traditions — and *at the level of historical context* — because they appropriate those various formal and
traditional elements in different contexts.

These are the basic elements that generally have come
under consideration in the practice of historical-critical
exegesis as that discipline has developed in the last two
hundred years. However, taken by themselves, they do not
provide a sufficient framework for interpreting the New
Testament. The reason is that much of the New Testament is polemical or at least hortatory in force. That is,
many New Testament writings are trying to correct or to
modify other people's understanding of the true nature of
the Jewish and Christian traditions and their applicability
to specific situations. The process of passing on a tradition
is always at the same time a process of (re)defining that
tradition, of locating the center of the tradition, and distin-
guishing that center from the peripheral and from what is
incompatible with the tradition. For example, both Paul and

his Galatian opponents are attempting to apply the story of Jesus and the Hebrew Bible to their specific situation. Unfortunately, they are coming to diametrically opposing conclusions. Thus it is not enough to speak of a traditional and literary/historical context. Another hermeneutical component must be added in order to understand the distinctive character of the New Testament writings. That component might be called an *interpretative matrix* — a set of implicit interpretative "rules" or assumptions by which a New Testament writer discriminates between what he regards as legitimate and illegitimate uses of Jewish and Christian traditions in any specific situational context. Such a matrix is the lens through which both context and tradition are viewed, and the implicit set of rules that govern the way tradition is brought to bear in a given context.

This hermeneutical component does not, however, necessarily bring us to a coherent center for the New Testament as a whole. It may well be that different New Testament writers operate with different sets of interpretative rules. Certainly Matthew has an interpretative approach that he applies to the Hebrew Bible that is quite different from that found in Hebrews, for example. Thus at one level, each New Testament text can be described as emerging from its own tradition, its own historical context, and its own hermeneutical or interpretative framework.

However, once we recognize that an understanding of the hermeneutical framework of a text is vital to its exegetical description and interpretation, another path is opened for finding new points of contact and convergence across New Testament documents. We are invited to search for points of contact and coherence among the New Testament documents, not only at the level of historical situations and shared traditions but also at the level of shared hermeneutical frameworks and structures. That is, in our search for a dynamic approach to the coherence of the New Testament, we may be helped by exploring the implicit forms of logic and shared assumptions that both energize and regulate the phenomenon of early Christianity.

In fact, the New Testament canon invites just this sort of inquiry across the whole range of New Testament documents. These documents together represent a body of literature that is distinct, both from the contemporary Jewish literature and from other texts we find in the Hellenistic world, despite many points of contact between the New Testament and these other bodies of literature. This distinctiveness is not adequately described by appeal only to historical situation (first-century religious texts), nor to a distinctive tradition (Jewish texts interested in Jesus), nor to common formal characteristics. There is something more here. What is it that makes the New Testament, at least in some basic sense, not only a distinctive body of literature but also a distinctive mode of religious discourse? If this is at all a meaningful question, we may be justified in seeking, across the range of New Testament documents, a larger and more general interpretative matrix that these writers share together, one that gives the New Testament as a whole its characteristic tone, emphasis, and dynamism. Of course, the seeking does not guarantee that we will find such a general interpretative matrix. Yet I would argue that the quest is at least invited, both by the New Testament documents themselves and by their collection into a canon of Scripture.

I suggest that when we begin to inquire into this interpretative matrix, we are inquiring into the basic character of the *gospel*. We find frequently in the New Testament that the writers operate with an awareness of a central message that shapes and directs their discourse as a whole and their appropriation and adaptation of tradition in particular. This is clearest when we look at the way New Testament writers interpret the Old Testament. One can conceivably use stories from the Hebrew Bible to speak of many different kinds of religious consciousness. However, the New Testament writers are explicit in their insistence that the Hebrew Bible be read "in light of Christ." For the New Testament writers, the gospel of Christ provides a hermeneutical vantage point from which the Hebrew Bible can be "properly" understood — that is, from which it can be understood from a distinctively *Christian* perspective.

However, it is not only the Hebrew Bible that, according to the New Testament, must be interpreted in light of the gospel. Stories about Jesus, Christian hymns, and Christian confessional materials must also be interpreted within this matrix. This is precisely what the four Gospels in the New Testament try to do. They create a new literary form by placing the stories about Jesus in an interpretative context that will illumine what the writer believes to be their true significance and meaning. Mark, for example, insists that we do not know what it means to acclaim Jesus as "Son of God" or "Messiah" unless we put these titles in the context of the suffering and crucifixion of Jesus. Likewise Paul insists that the Galatians' approach to Jesus as the Messiah threatens, ironically enough, to violate "the truth of the gospel" (Gal. 2:5, 14). One can tell stories about Jesus, sing

hymns, and confess faith, calling people to believe, and yet
be in complete contradiction to the gospel, at least as Paul
sees it.

Therefore, if we are to find an interpretative matrix that
effectively renders the distinctive character of the New Testament documents, we must consider the possibility that
what the New Testament calls "the gospel" may be the
key to identifying that matrix. This way of conceptualizing the nature of the gospel poses the question of the
coherence and distinctive character of the New Testament
more sharply. Specifically, it is a particular writer's understanding of the gospel that provides the discriminating
rules by which tradition and situation can be meaningfully
and "Christianly" brought together. This approach can be
diagrammed in the manner found in Figure 1.

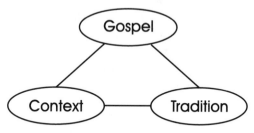

Figure 1:
A Model for Interpreting the New Testament

In each New Testament document, the contextual and
traditional dimensions of the document exist in a dynamic
interaction with each other. That interaction is also shaped

and regulated by the gospel, understood as an overall interpretative matrix, a comprehensive and synthetic vision for what Christian faith entails.

This way of looking at the New Testament carries within itself the possibility for a contemporary hermeneutic that itself grows from Scripture. If it is possible to uncover and render explicit that interpretative matrix by which the New Testament writers sifted, articulated, and appropriated the ongoing flood of Jewish and Christian traditions in new situations, it may well be that an analogous interpretative matrix can provide at least some clues for how we are to do the same today. In other words, I am proposing an approach to interpreting the New Testament that is concerned not only with describing and interpreting the *content* of the various New Testament documents. I am suggesting that our interpretation must make explicit the religious logic and implicit assumptions that governed the selection of traditional elements and the ways in which the historical contexts were addressed. As we recover that logic and those assumptions, we may be guided in how we are now to make use of the traditions recorded in Scripture as they are now brought to bear in new historical contexts.

"Gospel" as a Hermeneutical Structure

In what follows, I offer a preliminary attempt at defining further this interpretative matrix that governs and shapes the interaction of traditional and contextual elements. It must be noted before beginning, however, that this probe must necessarily have a tentative and preliminary status with respect to its integrative range. The overall interpretative matrix that I will articulate here is not fully reflected in all the New Testament writings. Significant aspects of the matrix are not developed or made explicit in some New Testament documents. I have already observed that the various New Testament documents do not operate with identical hermeneutical structures or assumptions. Nevertheless, I hope to delineate a clustering of shared hermeneutical structures and assumptions, centered around the New Testament category of "gospel," that operate across a wide range of New Testament documents. Obviously, the case for the gospel as hermeneutic needs to be established by a careful exegesis of the whole range of New Testament writings, a task that extends far beyond the scope of this study. But I offer at least a suggestive model that may serve as a starting point for further investigation and a catalyst for a creative and pluralist dialogical encounter with the New Testament. In the following chapter, I will illustrate how this model operates with regard to a particular question of contextuality within the New Testament.

How does one describe something like a hermeneutical structure? And how might one determine the hermeneutical structure of a given biblical text or collection of texts? I suggest that we take our cue from the New Testament writers who adopted the term *gospel* (εὐγγέλιον) to express their basic hermeneutical assumptions. The New Testament's use of this term invites three avenues of exploration. First, we need to come to understand why New Testament writers chose this particular term as a way to articulate the heart of their faith. This line of inquiry leads us to explore the semantic range and linguistic function of the word *gospel* in first century Mediterranean culture generally. Such exploration may help us in identifying some of the assumptions and presuppositions implicit in the use of the term *gospel*. Second, we must identify as clearly as possible the basic content of the gospel as the New Testament articulates it. What are the common themes, images, or motifs that characterize the New Testament's understanding of the gospel? Finally, we need to determine how the notion of "gospel" functions hermeneutically. That is to say, how can the New Testament's understanding of the gospel provide us with insight into the implicit logic and assumptions that energize and regulate the expressions of faith we find recorded in the New Testament?

The Term *Gospel*

The very choice of the term *gospel* (εὐγγέλιον) already gives us some insight into the nature and character of the faith that gave birth to the New Testament. Perhaps the most striking thing about the term is that it evokes an association with what we as moderns call "news." Usually it refers more specifically to "good news"; but even when the news is not good, in its usage outside the New Testament the term almost always refers to some message that comes as "news" or "announcement" to those who hear it. It can refer to the news of victory in war, or to someone's accession to kingship, or even to more mundane announcements like the birth of a son or news of an approaching wedding.

The choice of this term to articulate something central about Christian faith becomes more significant when one contemplates the alternatives that were being used in this period to express the essence of religious faith and experience. In articulating the essential character of its faith, early Christianity could have adopted one of the terms commonly used in the Hellenistic religious world such as *illumination* (φωτισμός), or *knowledge* (γνῶσις), or *mystery* (μυστήριον). Each of these terms appears in the New Testament as a designation for Christian faith. However, none of these terms acquires the widespread and generic status of the term *gospel*. One might observe that, in contrast to these other categories, the term *gospel* has a distinctly public character; it identifies Christian faith as news that has significance for all people, indeed for the whole world, not merely as esoteric understanding or insight, even though New Testament faith may have at times esoteric dimensions.

Early Christianity might also have continued the legacy of its Jewish heritage, referring to its newly emerging faith as *law* or *Torah* (νόμος), *instruction* (διδαχή), or *wisdom* (σοφία). As with the other Hellenistic terms we noted above, we also find the New Testament using this Jewish terminology to articulate its faith, but these terms also lack the widespread, generic character of "gospel" in the New Testament. The dimension of meaning that the term *gospel* adds to these other Jewish formulations is the event-oriented element of "news." The use of the term *gospel* in Koiné Greek generally does not suggest at its core the transmission of universal truths, principles, values, or wisdom (though these are not excluded), but rather focuses attention on the reporting of an event or happening of special significance: a victory in battle, an accession to kingship, or a political accomplishment.

The Content of the Gospel

If we press further, in order to delineate the specific content of the gospel in the New Testament, we encounter some difficulty. Different New Testament writers articulate the central message of Christian faith in different ways. For Paul, the gospel means that Gentiles are not required to undergo circumcision. Therefore Paul insists in Galatians that for Gentiles to receive circumcision is an abandonment of the gospel. In the Synoptic Gospels, by contrast, Jesus is depicted as proclaiming the gospel, but the message focuses on the coming reign of God. In the Book of Acts, the proclamation of the gospel seems closely related to the promise of forgiveness of sins. Even the most cursory review of the New Testament suggests that the gospel can be articulated in many different ways.

Yet even in the midst of that diversity, one detects common concerns and emphases as well. James D. G. Dunn identifies three motifs that are present throughout early Christian preaching: the proclamation of the risen, exalted Jesus; the call for faith; and a promise (grace, mercy, forgiveness, salvation, etc.) held out to faith (Dunn 1977:30). Although space precludes a fuller treatment here, I would add to Dunn's list the observation that almost all expressions of the gospel touch in some way upon the identity of Jesus and his death.[2] Hence, in the midst of substantial diversity in articulating the gospel, it seems clear that for New Testament writers, the gospel is always tied up with the identity, death, and resurrection of Jesus of Nazareth, a story that is announced as an act of God that offers a hopeful promise for the whole world. The New Testament finds its point of departure in the conviction that the identity of Jesus and his death and resurrection is "news" of public significance that needs to be told.

This emphasis in the New Testament on the centrality and public significance of the person of Jesus and his death and resurrection can be found even where the term *gospel* does not occur. In the Gospel of John, for example, even though the words for "proclaim the gospel" (εὐαγγελίζομαι and "gospel" (εὐγγέλιον) are not found in the body of the work, the universal and public significance of the person of Jesus and his death and resurrection, is clearly presupposed in the entire presentation of the story.

Furthermore, it is quite clear throughout the New Testament that Jesus' identity, death, and resurrection have *saving* significance. The religion of the New Testament is preeminently a religion of *salvation* (σωτηρία). It promises good news for the poor, forgiveness for the sinner, wholeness for the body, freedom, joy, hope, and eternal life. This soteriological dimension is in keeping with the prevailing use of the "gospel" word group (εὐαγγέλιον, εὐγγελίζομαι) in Koiné Greek. These words are commonly associated with "salvation" (σωτηρία) and "good fortune" (εὐτυχία, εὐτύχημα) (Friedrich 1965:711). The various New Testament writers of course differ at points on exactly what "salvation" means in concrete terms, but they share the assumption that their religion is a religion of salvation. The "salvation" word group (σωτηρία, σῴζω, σωτήρ) occupies an important place in every New Testament writer's vocabulary.

To summarize the discussion to this point, we have observed that the New Testament's designation of its faith as "gospel" suggests that New Testament faith centers around the public announcement of the story of Jesus' identity, death, and resurrection as a story of salvation. To put it differently, at the center of New Testament faith is the conviction that in the life, death, and resurrection of Jesus, God has revealed the completion of a saving purpose for the world, to be received by faith. Or we might use Paul's words in 2 Corinthians 5:19: "In Christ God was reconciling the world to himself."[3]

Of course, not every New Testament writer's work is equally derived from this kind of core formulation. However, the generic character of the term *gospel* invites us to consider this formulation as a kind of working model for the coherence of the New Testament, a model that we may further refine or qualify once the basic conceptual groundwork has been laid.

How "Gospel" Functions as a Hermeneutical Structure

In such a bare-bones formulation there is a large amount of room for widely divergent interpretations and applications. This high level of generality is necessary if the model is to be able to function across a wide range of New Testament writings. But this level of generality does not, in my opinion, render such summaries useless. If I am correct, a summary of "the gospel" like this is not intended to be a basic set of propositions from which the rest of Christian faith is *deduced*. It is too general for that. Rather, this summary of the gospel provides the hermeneutical perspective or matrix by which the convergence of tradition and specific historical context is *interpreted*.

How can this gospel summary function as a hermeneutical matrix or structure? I would suggest that almost every allusion to the gospel exhibits or implies a number of basic structural features: (1) The gospel always manifests itself as that which makes a claim that summons to allegiance and decision. In its insistence that the identity and career of Jesus Christ is of central soteriological significance, the gospel challenges people to accept the truth of that assertion and to modify their lives accordingly. The gospel is always that which is preached, the kerygma. Hence we may also say that the gospel is intimately associated with the experience of transformed perception and action. (2) The gospel presupposes a public horizon of interpretation — a horizon that is seen most clearly in apocalyptic literature, where the question of the relationship between the divine and the whole world is of central importance. It is "news." When we are dealing with interpretations governed by the gospel, it is always, finally, the world as a whole, the public world, with which God is dealing. This universal scope prevents the divine claim discussed above from becoming individualistic in orientation. The gospel envisions nothing less than God's action in the entire cosmos. In a sense, one might say that this cosmic horizon of interpretation is simply entailed in the notion of monotheism. If there is only one God, then language about such a God must necessarily encompass a universal frame of reference. (3) The gospel always presents this call to allegiance and universal scope in the context of the religious realities disclosed by the death and resurrection of Christ, which is regarded as paradigmatic for understanding the relationship between God and the world. One might say that this assumption assumes that the Christ event is revelatory in an ultimate or basic way. This is not to say that one can speak the gospel only when one is talking about Jesus. Rather, the Christ event provides the interpretative matrix by which the entire tradition takes form and meaning. At the barest minimum, this suggests that the death of Jesus provides some kind of definitive glimpse into the nature and character of the human predicament and deliverance from it, and the resurrection of Jesus provides some kind of definitive perspective on God's involvement with and attestation of Jesus' life and death.

What then is the gospel? In simplest terms, it is the proclamation of God's soteriological purpose and claim on this world, a purpose and claim extended paradigmatically through the crucified and risen Christ. Yet in the final analysis, this is not so much *what* is preached but rather the structure that delineates *how* the entire tradition is to be preached and interpreted.

Each of these basic structural elements of the gospel can and must be elaborated further. In particular, we must explore how a hermeneutical approach to the gospel such as the one we are advocating gives rise to theological and religious discourse and action. First, it must be recalled that the gospel is fundamentally *kerygmatic* in nature. To use the categories of speech-act theory developed by J. L. Austin, the proclaiming of the gospel is not only a *locutionary act,* conveying information, but an *illocutionary act,* calling forth some specific response from the hearer/reader. The gospel is language that not only conveys information but seeks to *bring about* a new state of affairs. Just as the words "I do" in the wedding service do more than simply describe the psychological state of the bride and groom at that particular time, so the announcement and acceptance of the gospel entails a reorientation of life in trust and obedience.

If the gospel is paradigmatic — if it is to provide a hermeneutical perspective from which to approach tradition and situation — then the gospel requires that the Christian tradition be articulated and lived in such a way that it makes a *claim* on the hearer. Central to the gospel is the notion that God is not detached or inert but is in search of human beings and, given the apocalyptic coordinates of the gospel, the world as a whole. The gospel in a basic sense represents the call of God to which the world in general, and humans in particular, is called to respond. Moreover, this call is a radical claim on life in its totality. Hence the response of faith is to confess that Jesus is *Lord* — that God's universal claim over this world in Christ is valid.

This universal claim over the world manifests itself paradigmatically in the Christ event, God's reign, which discloses a dialectical interaction between death and resurrection, mercy and judgment, radical renunciation and pity for the weak. Because God extends a claim over the world, God can be known to *love* the world, to desire that it be all that it should be. The same is true of individuals and societies. This is the hope conveyed in the resurrection of Jesus. And yet, the very fact that God *extends* God's claim in Christ suggests that this claim is not universally acknowledged, that there is resistance to God's claim, a resistance graphically portrayed in the crucifixion of Jesus. Hence the Christian tradition is interpreted and applied Christianly when God's claim on life is presented dialectically, both in judgment and mercy, in affirmation and critique, in embrace and in the call to repentance.

Finally, the Christian tradition is interpreted and applied in accordance with the gospel when the present *need* for a restoration to a right relationship with God's sovereign claim is juxtaposed with an affirmation of God's *action* to bring this about. The gospel insists that the Christian tradition be interpreted in such a way as to affirm that God is in the process of "making good" on the divine claim to the world and that this process has come to its climax in the Christ event. Hence there is a characteristic dimension of *hope* and *trust* that is an essential component of a distinctively Christian rendering of the tradition — a hope and trust that are specifically attached to and that grow from the stories about Jesus. One tells the stories about Jesus Christianly when one tells them in such a way that they elicit the response of hope and trust in the God who is revealed in them.

But who is the God who is revealed in the tradition and in the stories about Jesus? Our simple structural approach to the gospel does not and cannot tell us much. God is that which makes a claim on the world, a claim that manifests itself dialectically in judgment and mercy, a claim that does not deny present suffering but generates hope. Yet this is only an abstract picture.

It is here that a narrative approach to the biblical texts must find a place in one's overall construal of the distinctive character of the biblical message. The naked structure of the gospel can never exist in isolation; its general symbolic structure must always be given specific content by the richness of the narrative texture of the tradition. The content we pour into the words God and Jesus spoken of in our interpretative matrix are the identities that are rendered by the cumulative impact of the many narratives about God and Jesus within Scripture. The interpretative matrix cannot survive apart from the traditions that it interprets.

However, the interpretative matrix of the gospel does provide some parameters that delineate a context by which even the specific narratives of Scripture may be read and understood. Thus, for example, the public dimensions of the gospel in its basic structural shape preclude the narrowly sectarian reading of the biblical narrative we find in the theology of apartheid.

In other words, the gospel functions to bring about a fundamental transformation in the way people in a specific situation interpret the Christian tradition, understand themselves, and situate themselves in their world as a whole. An old mode of self-understanding and orientation must die and a new one come to birth. In a sense, the gospel is intended to function for the totality of perception and self-understanding in the same way that a specific metaphor functions within a limited range of perception and self-understanding. Just as a metaphor juxtaposes two disparate images in order to disclose a deeper way of perceiving and understanding in a specific domain of awareness, so too the root images implicit in the gospel, when juxtaposed both against the Christian tradition and against a specific situation, disclose a new and all-encompassing mode of self-understanding and orientation.

Conclusion

Obviously, much more could be said, but this is at least a beginning. If this approach is to be borne out and established by exegesis, however, it means that we must always be asking three basic questions in our reading of the New Testament: (1) What is the specific situation that prompts this writing and to which it is addressed? (2) How are the Jewish and Christian traditions being brought to bear in this specific situation? (3) What are the hermeneutical assumptions that guide this bringing together of tradition and situation in literary form, and how are these assumptions related to basic Christian affirmations about the center of the gospel? The more these questions dominate our reading of Scripture, the more our reading of the Bible will bring us back, again and again, to the center of the New Testament and of Christian faith. And the closer we come to that center, the more focused will be our own missiological understanding. There is a *truth* that we speak in love, a gospel that both sanctions and constrains our diverse expressions of faith. The clearer we are about the nature and character of that gospel, the more empowered we will be to speak the truth in love.

In the following chapter, we will illustrate how these interactions between gospel, tradition, and context can be helpful in exploring a particular issue in New Testament interpretation. We will also explore the linkages between these issues in New Testament theology and the broader missiological questions that form the backdrop of this study.

4

A Case Study:
Christians and Roman Rule

We turn now to a specific example in order to illustrate the previous chapter's observations about the New Testament's hermeneutical structure. We will look at a specific topic on which various New Testament writers adopted contrasting positions — the attitude Christians should adopt with regard to the Roman Empire and its rule. We will explore not only how and why these writers differed from each other but also how those differences may indicate diverse ways in which the gospel can come to bear in different contexts. We will explore texts from Paul, Luke-Acts, the Gospel According to John, and the Apocalypse. In each case, we will examine contextual and traditional elements, looking particularly at how these elements are brought together in light of the gospel as a hermeneutical structure.

We will discover as we look at these specific passages that each writer does reflect a bringing together of tradition and situation in light of the gospel. However, the writers do not all do it in the same way, and they come to views of the Roman Empire that are in some respects incompatible with each other. Some of this incompatibility may be due to differing contexts in which the various writers are located or to differing aspects of the Christian tradition on which they draw. At other more fundamental points, the differences may lie in different ways in which the gospel functions as a hermeneutical matrix. As we explore these differences, we will also attempt to bring these passages into conversation with each other for the purpose of mutual critique. We will try to demonstrate that even though the writers attempt to interpret their situations in light of the gospel, their interpretations are always provisional and contextual, subject to widening and deepening in the light of conversations with other contexts. The gospel as a hermeneutical matrix is not exhausted by any single writer's application of it to a specific context or tradition. The "canonical conversation" among these various New Testament texts helps to disclose a larger and more encompassing frame of reference constituted by the gospel, in which each of these texts may be more deeply interpreted.

In the following chapter, we will explore how the canonical conversation among these texts may serve as a model for missiological conversations between Christians from diverse contexts, and between Christians and their own contexts. In so doing, we hope to show how the resources of the New Testament can illumine missiological interpretation today.

Paul's Advice on Responsibilities to Rulers: Romans 13:1–7

This is a passage that bristles with hermeneutical difficulties. First, the somewhat vague and general language of the text is surprising. Despite the fact that this is Paul's letter "to the Romans," there is no explicit mention of Rome nor of the emperor. All the references are to "rulers" in the plural or to a more abstract "authority." Hence it is unclear whether Paul is speaking specifically about the context of Christians in Rome and their particular struggles with local rulers or about the relation between Christians and governance generally.

It is also unclear whether we should construe Paul's remarks as pastoral advice to the Romans or as a slightly defensive presentation of his own "view" on the relationship of Christianity to governance. In the first case, the passage would attempt to shed light on an issue that may have been the source of contention and confusion among Roman Christians. In the second case, it may be that the Roman Christians were not troubled at all in their attitude toward Rome, but that Paul feared they were suspicious of him because of his various scrapes with Roman administrators on his journeys. Paul then could be understood as defending himself against a suspicion of political subversion.

Finally, many commentators have puzzled over the rosy portrait of governing authorities that emerges from these verses. Paul speaks of rulers as "not a terror to good conduct, but to bad" (13:3). He speaks of the authority as "God's servant for your good" (13:4, 6). Paul was certainly aware of (and had experienced) incidents in which Roman rulers acted as a terror to good conduct rather than to bad. One needs to think only of Pontius Pilate's role in the crucifixion of Jesus. Yet this passage seems to ascribe an unqualified divine approval to rulers who, even in the best of circumstances, reflect the divine will only partially in their actions.

A consideration of the literary context of this passage may help to overcome some of these difficulties. This passage is best understood as a further explication of 12:14–21, especially 12:18: "If it is possible, so far as it depends on you, live peaceably with all." Paul's comments in chapter 12 make it quite clear that he does not believe that the Christian obligation to love is conditioned upon the behavior of the one who is loved. Rather, Christians must love even their enemies and overcome evil with good (12:20–21, 13:8). The language of "overcoming evil with good" readily calls to mind Paul's discussion of the death of Jesus, in which Jesus' loving allegiance to God's purpose is announced as the ultimate victory over evil (e.g., Rom 5:6–8). Thus the loyalty to rulers in chapter 13 flows from the example of Jesus alluded to in chapter 12. Therefore the question of whether rulers always act appropriately as God's servants is immaterial to Paul's argument.

At the same time, Paul might have realized, on further reflection, that 13:3 is just not always true. This rhetorical flourish may be an attempt on Paul's part to present himself as a loyal citizen who believes in the system and does not intend to subvert it. Yet it appears to overstate the case and subverts, to some extent, the line of argument in chapter 12, on which this discussion appears to be built.

Moreover, the use of the plural "rulers" suggests that Paul is not concerned with "Christianity and the state" as a general problem, nor with the Roman government as a whole, but rather with the concrete, face-to-face relations between Christians and local governing authorities. This also suggests that Paul is not merely trying to prove that he is not a revolutionary, but also that he is trying to work out an ethical position to commend to the Roman Christians.[4] The general point seems to be that one's obligations toward others, including governing authorities, must be grounded in the same faithful, vulnerable love shown to us by God in Christ (12:1–2). Although Paul may make some implicit critique of Roman power at some other points in his letters, he does not engage that issue here.[5]

What then shall we make of this text hermeneutically? Paul clearly makes use of some earlier Christian traditions, particularly Jesus' words about loving one's enemies (Matt. 5:44; Luke 6:27). His words have a contextualized element; he seems to be at some pains to remove any suspicion that his gospel is engaged in political subversion of the empire and also to provide specific guidance to Christians in their everyday experience. There is a clear sense in which these contextual and traditional elements are brought together in light of the gospel: the nonviolent death of Jesus provides a graphic example of overcoming evil with good, and of how submission to governing authority, even when it appears to be arbitrary, violent, and evil, can issue in the furthering of God's will and purpose.

What seems out of keeping with the structure of the gospel is the unqualified approval given to governing authorities. Certainly the story of Jesus' death and resurrection suggests that governing authorities can unwittingly aid the purposes of God, even when their actions are evil and unjust. Yet there is little in the story of Jesus or in the larger biblical story to support Paul's contention that "rulers are not a terror to good conduct, but to bad." It appears that at this point, Paul's rhetoric may have been politically necessary, but it still appears to be wishful thinking and not directly supportable by the hermeneutical framework of the gospel, which portrays human behavior, not first of all as the reflection of God's justice, but as resistance to that justice — a resistance that is only overcome in Christ. Paul's language here may reflect God's intention for governance, as is evidenced in the New Testament's depiction of the lordship of Jesus (cf. Phil. 2:5–11). That is, Paul may be thinking of what *should* be, rather than what *is*. If that is the case, however, the grammar of the text does not reflect this, for Paul's actual language is in an indicative, rather than hortatory, mood.

Our analysis of Romans 13 therefore provides both a window of understanding into the basic logic and structure of the passage and also a critical perspective by which the passage can be assessed. Paul's use of the gospel illumines the way he addresses his context in light of the Christian tradition. Yet Paul's use of the gospel does not exhaust its potential, and there are some points where Paul's context seems to obscure certain aspects of the gospel.

It is at this point that a canonical conversation becomes critical. Because Paul's address to the Roman Christians is so contextualized, it needs to be brought into conversation with other New Testament documents if the full scope of the gospel as an overall hermeneutical framework is to be discerned. Hence the critical perspective that we have begun to adopt in our review of Romans 13 must be further sharpened by considering the perspective of other New Testament passages.

Jesus Before Pilate: Luke 23:1–25

We turn next to Jesus' trial before Pilate, as recorded in the Gospel According to Luke, in order to explore the interaction of traditional and contextual elements in light of the gospel. It has become commonplace in Lucan scholarship to note that Luke seems to go out of his way to portray Roman authorities in a positive light and as benevolently disposed toward Christians. Roman soldiers are consistently portrayed as peaceable upholders of the public good (see, e.g., the centurion Cornelius in Acts 10). Roman officials investigating charges of misconduct against Christians almost always find that the charges are false. In Acts 18:12–17, Gallio, the proconsul of Achaia, dismisses all charges against Paul as "a matter of questions about words and names and your own law." In Acts 23:26ff., the tribune Claudius Lysias writes about Paul to the governor Felix: "I found that he was accused concerning questions of their law, but was charged with nothing deserving death or imprisonment." Later Festus, the governor replacing Felix, declares to King Agrippa, "This man is doing nothing to deserve death or imprisonment," to which Agrippa replies, "This man could have been set free if he had not appealed to the emperor" (Acts 26:31–32).

These same motifs removing Christians from any conflict with Rome are present in the trial of Jesus before Pilate in Luke 23:1–25. Three times Pilate declares that Jesus is innocent (23:4, 14, 22). The same affirmation comes from the centurion's lips after Jesus dies (Luke 23:47). This is all the more significant, in light of the initial charge that is brought against Jesus only in the Lucan account: "We found

this man perverting our nation, forbidding us to pay taxes
to the emperor, and saying that he himself is the Messiah,
a king" (Luke 23:2). The entire narrative exonerates Jesus
of any charge related to subversion of the Roman Empire.
It is Jewish hostility that brings about Jesus' crucifixion, not
Roman law (Luke 23:23). The Jews ironically demand instead that Barabbas be released, whom Luke identifies as "a
man who had been put in prison for an insurrection that
had taken place in the city, and for murder" (Luke 23:19).

The passage as a whole may contain an implicit criticism of Pilate for failing to act on his own judgment of
innocence and allowing the crowd to have its way. Pilate's
offer to scourge Jesus and release him in Luke 23:16 also
seems unwarranted. This behavior of Pilate is in keeping with Luke's portrayal of other Roman officials, who at
times mistreat Christians, even though they acknowledge
Christians' innocence.[6] Luke is not so much interested in
exculpating Roman officials as he is in exculpating Christians. Nevertheless, the clear message of the trial, when
taken as a whole, is that Jesus posed no threat to Rome and
that his death was a miscarriage of justice.

It is, of course, a matter of great debate today whether
this is a historically accurate picture of the circumstances
surrounding Jesus' crucifixion. Some scholars argue that
Jesus did present himself as a political revolutionary of
sorts, particularly in his entry into Jerusalem and his
"cleansing of the temple," and that the Romans simply took
no chances in executing a potentially dangerous subversive.
Others argue that Jewish authorities were more directly involved and attempted to remove a troublesome religious
gadfly. But regardless of how one may decide such issues,

Luke's intention remains quite clear. The Roman Empire has nothing to fear from Jesus or his followers.

How are we to assess such an emphasis, in light of the hermeneutical model we have developed? Many scholars have noted that this positive portrayal of Rome fits in well with the apologetic tenor of much of Luke-Acts and its attempt to present the early church in terms that would be accessible and attractive to members of the Greco-Roman world, particularly to people of wealth. This context helps to shed light on the particular way in which the traditions of Jesus' trial and death are handled in Luke.

But what of the gospel? How has the larger story of Jesus' life, death, and resurrection as the culmination of God's saving purpose for the world shaped the portrayal of Jesus' engagement with the Roman Empire? In order to answer this question, we must first distinguish between Luke's particular *narrative* of the gospel story and "gospel" as the hermeneutical matrix that governs the way tradition and situation are brought together. Even though Luke is telling the gospel narrative, he is doing so in a particular way that reflects his own context and use of traditions. There is no noncontextualized telling of the gospel narrative. Yet in each telling of the narrative, we can look for the hermeneutical clues and assumptions that reveal the implicit rules governing the interaction of context and tradition, including the traditions about Jesus' death. In this way, a careful examination even of particular gospel *narratives* can provide us clues for how the gospel functions as an *interpretative matrix*.

Clearly, this passage attempts to relate one of the central components of the gospel story. Yet it relates the story in a particular fashion, shaped by the context and aims of the writer and readers. It is at precisely this point that some scholars fault Luke's presentation. They argue that Luke's refusal to allow the gospel story to criticize Rome in any way has resulted in such a spiritualized understanding of Jesus' kingship that the gospel no longer represents a divine saving purpose *for this world,* thereby recasting salvation into "religious" and completely otherworldly terms.[7] The loss of any critical perspective on the violence and oppression of the Roman Empire — the failure even to acknowledge clearly the basic fact that Rome crucified Jesus — results in a diminishing of the content and scope of the gospel. According to these scholars, the cosmic horizon of the gospel has narrowed in Luke's portrayal.

Yet this perspective may not tell the whole story about Luke's understanding of the public implications of the gospel. There are many passages in Luke and Acts in which there is a great deal of concern about poverty and oppression, and a translation of the gospel into "this-worldly" terms. Mary's *Magnificat* celebrates how God "has brought down the powerful from their thrones, and lifted up the lowly" (Luke 1:52). Luke alone includes the parable of the rich man and Lazarus (Luke 16:19–31), which portrays a wealthy man in torment for his failure to meet the needs of a poor beggar during his life. The story of the early Jerusalem church celebrates the sharing of possessions so that "there was not a needy person among them" (Acts 4:34).

Luke does show a great concern for the poor, a concern that flows directly from his understanding of the significance of Jesus' life, death, and resurrection. This becomes clear when Luke's discourse is viewed against the social background of patronage — the complex interaction of patrons, clients, and brokers that made up the social fabric of Luke's day. Jesus is portrayed as the broker of divine power, but not in such a way that his status increases. This places Jesus in dramatic contrast to the normal goals of patronage in the ancient world. The whole motive for patronage in the ancient world is to acquire greater fame and status — and therefore power — through generosity. Instead, Luke portrays Jesus as the "one who serves" (Luke 22:27). Luke portrays the typical client-patron relations of his day; but he calls for a radical redefinition of these relationships in which patrons no longer receive honor and status in return for their generosity, but instead assume the role of servants, expecting nothing in return (e.g., Luke 6:35; 9:46–48; 22:24–27) (Moxnes 1991:241–268). So Luke's understanding of the gospel does impact the social fabric of this world and is not confined to an other-worldly notion of salvation.

However, Luke's critique of patronage has potentially profound implications for the whole structure of the Roman Empire, which was deeply shaped by patronage in the basic fabric of its social relations, from the emperor on down (Moxnes 1991:244ff.). Yet Luke's apologetic agenda seems to prevent him from attempting to extend his understanding of the gospel's critique of patronage to a broader critique of the Roman Empire. For Luke, the Roman Empire's *pax Romana* functions only to provide the secure environment in which the new kind of benefaction he longs for can take place. Luke's context has led him to appropriate the tradition of Jesus' death in a selective manner that reflects, to varying degrees, the basic structures of the gospel. Although Luke's apologetic context has shaped his use of traditions without much concern for the basic structures of the gospel when he addresses Roman rule, Luke does use the more basic structures of the gospel to interpret other Greco-Roman social institutions on a smaller scale.

Jesus Before Pilate: John 18:28–19:16

We turn next to the trial of Jesus in the Gospel According to John, to see how the hermeneutical matrix of the gospel shapes the interaction of historical context and tradition. Already prior to this passage depicting Jesus' trial, the fourth evangelist has set a narrative context that focuses attention particularly on Rome's involvement in the arrest and trial of Jesus. David Rensberger (1988) has pointed out that we find only in John mention of a Roman cohort and its commander at Jesus' arrest (18:3, 11). By contrast, in the Synoptics it is only Jewish officials who arrest Jesus. In further contrast to the Synoptics, no Jewish court formally condemns Jesus, nor do the Jews administer any beating or mockery.[8] The center of gravity in John falls much more on Jesus' interaction with Pilate and with Roman officials than with the Jewish authorities. We do not find here the tendency we saw in Luke to shift the blame for Jesus' crucifixion away from Rome and onto "the Jews." John's interest seems to be focused on the engagement between Jesus and Pilate, the representative of Roman power, and only secondarily on the role of the Jews. It is Pilate, not the Jews, who appears in every scene.

Traditionally, Pilate is interpreted in this passage as a weak and sympathetic character who knows that Jesus is innocent, but Pilate capitulates to the wishes of the Jews in order to avoid trouble. David Rensberger (1988) has offered a compelling and dramatically different interpretation of Pilate, however. He suggests that the evangelist presents Pilate as a cynical and calculating figure who uses Jesus to humiliate and manipulate the Jews. After cynically rejecting Jesus' language about truth in 18:38, Pilate goes out and tells the Jews that he finds no case against Jesus, and offers to release "the King of the Jews." Such a way of referring to Jesus was bound to incense the Jews, and Rensberger suggests that this was its precise intent.

The fact that Pilate then proceeds to have Jesus flogged shows that Pilate is not centrally concerned with Jesus' innocence, for such action was forbidden by Roman law prior to the conviction of a crime. Pilate then brings out the bloody parody of a king in Jesus and says to the crowd, "Here is the man!" (19:15). When the crowd again demands crucifixion, Pilate tells them to take Jesus and crucify him themselves, although the reader already knows from 18:31 that this is impossible. The effect is simply to force the crowd to acknowledge that Pilate is the one in control of the situation.

When Pilate then hears that Jesus has claimed to be the Son of God, the text says μᾶλλον ἐφοβήθη, which can be translated either "he was more afraid than ever" or "he began to be afraid instead." The latter translation is to be preferred. Pilate for the first time actually considers Jesus' claims about himself, rather than focusing only on using him as a tool to manipulate the Jews. For the first time (in contrast to his feigned earlier remarks), Pilate actually tries to release Jesus (19:12a). Yet this attempt lasts only briefly.

When the Jews raise the issue of loyalty to the emperor in 19:12b, Pilate quickly reverts to his basic manipulative strategy. He brings Jesus out and seats him on the judge's bench, declaring to the Jews, "Here is your king!"[9] When the Jews respond "We have no king but the emperor" (19:15), Pilate achieves his basic objective and hands Jesus over for crucifixion.

Why is Pilate presented in such a fashion? Rensberger suggests that the evangelist is arguing for a third way, neither the path of armed Jewish resistance to Rome, like Barabbas (cf. 18:36), nor the path of passive acquiescence to Roman rule, like the Jewish authorities. Jesus' assertion "My kingdom is not from this world" (18:36) does not suggest that Jesus' kingdom has nothing to do with this world, but that it does not *originate* within the structures and assumptions of this world. Allegiance to Jesus' kingdom exposes the sad distance between Rome's rule and the divine purpose, as well as the violence of those who would seek to oppose Roman rule.[10] John spells out no alternative political strategy or program, but clearly sees the life, death, and resurrection of Jesus calling into question the validity both of Roman rule and of armed Jewish resistance. In the late first century, after the tragic failure of the first Jewish revolt as well as the brutality of Rome in suppressing that revolt, it was undoubtedly easier to note the failures than to propose comprehensive alternatives.

Yet John does propose an alternative of a sort, although it does not encompass the whole world: he proposes the politics of a gathered community, radically loyal to God's manifestation in Jesus Christ and willing to love and serve one another even to the point of death (13:1–20). The quasi-sectarian opposition between such communities and "the world" (e.g., 17:6ff.) might be construed as a limit on the public horizon of the basic gospel matrix. Yet John is ambivalent here, at times indicating that God's saving purpose extends to the whole world (e.g., 1:29; 3:16f.; 4:42; 6:33; 51; 8:12; 12:19; 47), and at other times, identifying the world as that which is resistant to and alienated from God's saving purpose (e.g, 1:10; 7:7; 8:23; 12:31; 14:17; 27; 15:18f.; 16:20; 17:9ff.). In contrast to both Paul and Luke, John is more willing to engage Roman rule in a critical fashion as he relates the gospel narrative. Yet that critical edge, itself an outworking of gospel assumptions, threatens to move John toward a sectarian posture that also runs the danger of losing the public horizon of the gospel. John's context of a Christianity experiencing sharp opposition, along with the exhaustion and despair that followed the Jewish revolt, must be taken into account in assessing these complex ways in which contextual and traditional elements are brought together in light of the gospel. John brings together the story of Jesus and his own situation in such a way that the critical edge of the gospel is heard clearly, but a more constructive side that embraces the whole world is only ambiguously present.

Rome as Babylon, Beast, and Whore: Revelation 18

Finally, we turn to the Book of Revelation, where a critical perspective on Roman rule is heard with the greatest force of any book in the New Testament. Even the most cursory reading of the Book of Revelation makes obvious the profound and thoroughgoing critique of Rome that dominates the book. Richard Bauckham summarizes it well:

> Revelation portrays the Roman Empire as a system of violent oppression, founded on conquest, maintained by violence and oppression. It is a system both of political tyranny and of economic exploitation. The two major symbols for Rome, which represent different aspects of the empire, are the sea-monster ('the beast': especially chapters 13 and 17) and the harlot of Babylon (especially chapters 17–18). The beast represents the military and political power of the Roman Emperors. Babylon is the city of Rome, in all her prosperity gained by economic exploitation of the Empire. Thus the critique in chapter 13 is primarily political, the critique in chapters 17–18 primarily economic, but in both cases also deeply religious. The beast and the harlot are intimately related. The harlot rides on the beast (17:3), because the prosperity of the city of Rome at the Empire's expense and her corrupting influence over the Empire rest on the power achieved and maintained by the imperial armies (Bauckham 1993:35–36).

The critique of Rome contained in these interlocking symbols comes to its climax in Revelation 18. In a sweeping and poetic vision of divine judgment against Babylon, the writer places into the mouths of those who profit by the Roman Empire a series of lamentations regarding all the luxury and beauty that is now lost. In a particularly dramatic sequence (vv. 11–13) is listed a whole series of exquisite and luxurious items that are now lost, culminating with the loss of "slaves — and human lives" (v. 13). This commodification of human life stands at the center of Revelation's critique of Rome and as the cause for its downfall.

It has often been assumed that Revelation is written to Christians undergoing persecution, to give them endurance through difficult times. That certainly seems to be the case for some of the recipients. However, if we take seriously the seven letters with which the book opens, it seems that more of the recipients of this book are suffering from complacency than from persecution. The writer excoriates his readers for their loss of first love (2:4), false teaching (Pergamum, 2:12–17) which accommodates to culture (food sacrificed to idols), loss of watchfulness (Sardis, 3:1–6), and being lukewarm (Laodicea, 3:14ff.). These are not the ills usually experienced by churches undergoing persecution! Hence the trend in more recent studies on Revelation is to conclude that at least part of the writer's intent is to *create* a sense of distance and alienation from Rome in the minds and hearts of Christians who are in danger of being seduced by Roman power and wealth, perhaps through participation in the imperial cult.

Therefore the call in 18:4 is "Come out of her, my people, so that you do not take part in her sins, and so that you do not share in her plagues." The writer tries to break the allure of Rome by the vision of its future downfall. He calls for a radical separation, not so much physical as intellectual, emotional, and spiritual. Christians must not receive "the mark of the beast" on themselves (16:2; 19:20).

At one level, this critique of Rome can be understood as growing directly out of fundamental aspects of the gospel narrative. Revelation regards Rome as the antithesis of many of the values exemplified in the life, death, and resurrection of Jesus, values such as nonviolence, concern for the poor and oppressed, economic justice, and mutuality. Rome is rightly challenged for falling short. Moreover, Revelation clearly maintains the cosmic horizon of the gospel narrative, addressing the question of divine sovereignty and justice over the entire world. The gospel has clear and profound implications for the kingdoms of this world.

What is less clear, however, is how the death and resurrection of Jesus is for Revelation an expression of God's saving purpose for the world. In Revelation, the death of Jesus is the paradigmatic martyr's death that atones for the sins of believers and ransoms them for God (1:5; 5:9). Yet it seems clear that God's *saving* purpose for the world is revealed in the series of judgments symbolically depicted by the book, rather than by the death of Jesus. The death and resurrection of Jesus saves individuals, in the sense of providing access to God and having their names written in the book of life (13:8; 17:8; 20:12ff.). But the salvation of the world, if one defines that as the setting right of the world, comes only in the seer's visions and seems only distantly related to the gospel matrix.

This dichotomy raises questions about whether Revelation thinks through far enough the implications of confessing the death and resurrection of Jesus as a saving event. It might be the case that if Revelation regarded the death and resurrection of Jesus not only as the salvation of individuals but also the salvation of the world, then it might be led to explore how that death and resurrection might lead Christians to transform life in this world as called for in Romans 12 and not merely patiently to await its destruction. Moreover, a fuller consideration of Jesus' own response to evil might have led the seer to consider with Paul whether evil exists not to be violently overcome but rather to be overcome with good (e.g., Rom. 12:21).

Revelation draws on many traditions, both of the Hebrew Bible and of early Christianity, to explore the gospel's claim that Jesus is the "ruler of the kings of the earth." Yet other aspects of the gospel matrix are not so clearly present, particularly those that see Jesus' death, as well as his resurrection, as central to God's saving purpose for the world.

Cross-contextual Conversation as a Resource

The preceding analysis of texts from Romans, Luke, John, and Revelation has shown substantial diversities, within the New Testament itself, on the question of the relationship of Christians to Roman rule. These diversities are illumined (though not always reconciled) by the various contexts from which they spring. These diversities make it difficult for Christians today to use the Bible to guide and shape their lives. If one simply approaches the New Testament as a smorgasbord table and picks and chooses as one wishes, Christians will not find the Bible a helpful source for the resolution of disputes. Simply laying out the options on the table provides no guidance as to how we should choose.

The missional hermeneutic proposed in this book provides a way to bring these various and diverse passages into conversation with each other, around a common framework. Our discussion has shown how each of these texts can be challenged and perhaps corrected or balanced by one of the others. Paul's rosy estimate of rulers' actions is balanced by the stark honesty of Revelation, and Revelation's call for vengeance is challenged by Romans' plea for purposive, nonviolent action. Luke's call for economic justice and for a critique of patronage can be affirmed, while at the same time recognizing that the critique may extend further than Luke takes it, as John and Revelation clearly show.

Our survey thus suggests that there is both a synthetic and a critical function to the missional hermeneutic we have developed, when it is applied across the New Testament canon as a whole. At the synthetic level, each passage contributes to our overall understanding of the gospel matrix. At the critical level, the diversities of articulation also call attention to the limited way in which each passage brings the gospel to bear hermeneutically. The delineation of gospel as a hermeneutical matrix therefore requires not simply adding up the variety of testimonies to the gospel but also bringing them into a critical conversation with each other. Such a perspective coheres nicely with our earlier observations regarding the dynamic interaction between particularity and universality in a missional hermeneutic. Just as local Christian communities must find their own ways of expressing the gospel in their context and yet must also discover in the gospel the clues to their common humanity and faith in conversation with others, so also the various New Testament passages evidence their particular contextuality, but also their common witness to the gospel, when brought into conversation with each other in the canon.

This is not to say that a hermeneutic such as we have developed will resolve all tensions into some perfectly balanced dialectical approach. It is interesting that we see no such perfectly balanced dialectic in the New Testament itself. Rather, what we see are Christians seeking to find wisdom in the basic gospel narratives that will guide them in making sense of the world around them and the traditions that form their memories. If the New Testament is our guide, Christians always do so in limited and provisional ways. However, when the diverse New Testament perspectives are brought into conversation with each other, within the context of the canon as a whole, some illumining perspectives emerge that deepen our insight into the basic gospel message and its implications for a variety of specific contexts.

Likewise, when Christians today find themselves differing, sometimes radically, in the way they apply the gospel to their lives, the practice of conversation in the whole church around questions of context, tradition, and gospel provides the opportunity for each to deepen understanding into the mysterious story that shapes all our lives.

It is not the purpose of this survey to come to explicit conclusions regarding the relationship between Christianity and the state. The diversity among the texts we surveyed makes a single answer that is valid in all contexts impossible. Moreover, that very diversity within the canon cautions against any attempt to make one "view" of "the state" a necessary corollary of the gospel itself. Yet the hermeneutical model developed here can provide some tools for self-criticism regarding the way we bring together tradition and context in our expressions of Christian faith. Moreover, the model can provide a starting point for reflection with other Christians from other contexts by focusing upon the common commitments and values that Christians share without suppressing the diversity that is part of the divine purpose for human life. The next chapter seeks to make explicit how such a model might function in contemporary missiological conversations.

5

Contemporary Use
of a Missional Hermeneutic

Developing a Model
for Missiological Interpretation

The interaction we have discerned in the New Testament between context, tradition, and gospel provides helpful guidance for contemporary missiological reflection. Every act of interpreting and living Christian faith is, in essence, a repetition of the kind of activity the biblical writers did themselves when they sat down to write. As interpreters, we find ourselves in a specific historical, social, and cultural context, and we struggle to find meaning within that context. We too wrestle with the religious traditions that give us our identity. Those traditions include the biblical documents but also many other traditions: our confessions, hymnody, rituals, forms of worship, and the like.

However, if we are to interpret the New Testament properly and live out the faith expressed in it, there must also be another factor in our interpretative performances — an awareness of the dynamics and structure of the gospel. The more clearly we are aware of how the gospel functions hermeneutically within the New Testament documents, the more clearly we will be able to embody that same framework within our own interpretations of the Bible and expressions of faith.

I believe that an understanding of the hermeneutical function of the gospel is critical to a healthy approach to plurality and coherence in biblical interpretation and the broader task of missiological interpretation. Interpretation will always emerge out of different contexts. There will always be different traditions brought to bear in different ways by various interpreters. However, in the midst of all this diversity, the gospel can function as a framework that invites conversation and lends a sense of coherence and commonality in the midst of such wide diversity. Such a framework does not suppress our diversity but enables us to discover our common humanity and our common faith, in the midst of our diversity.

In order to clarify how this framework should function, let us return to the graphic image of this model used in Chapter 3. There we suggested that each New Testament document represented a convergence of context, tradition, and gospel.

If this model is to function in contemporary missiological reflection (see Figure 2 on the following page), it requires a certain form of analysis and a certain kind of conversation. It requires, first, that we analyze our present expressions of Christian faith using these categories. What aspects of our expressions of Christian faith are drawn from the Christian tradition, both in Scripture and in the history of the church? What aspects are distinctively shaped by our

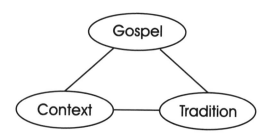

Figure 2:
A Model For Missiological Interpretation

own context? And how are the interactions between our tradition and our context shaped by our understanding of the core narrative of the gospel?

Once these elements have been identified, they can be sharpened and illumined by conversations with Christians from other contexts. Those conversations often reveal ways in which our own context has unconsciously shaped our understanding of the gospel and our use of the Christian tradition. The result may be a broader understanding of the resources of the Christian tradition as well as a deeper understanding of hermeneutical implications of the gospel of which we were previously unaware.

A variety of other results may ensue from such conversations as well. They can lead us to a deeper understanding of our own context and to a form of Christian faith and life more directly relevant to and grounded in our own context. They may also lead to a deeper recognition and appreciation for the diverse ways in which Christian faith takes root in diverse contexts. But perhaps the most sought-for result is a deepening grasp of the gospel itself. For the gospel is not merely some critically assured minimum confession that we share with all Christians. It is rather that metanarrative or charter story that shapes our lives at the deepest level as Christians. The more deeply and broadly we reflect upon this basic matrix, the more effectively we can interpret both our context and our tradition with insight and power.

Conclusion

In conclusion, we return to the questions with which we began: What does it mean to be called to speak of the gospel as *truth* in a world that declares that religious speech can never be true but only "true-for-you"? How can we speak the truth from a posture of loving servanthood in a world that interprets truth claims as political strategies masking inevitable self-interests? And finally, what is the role of Scripture in leading us to the truth and in teaching us how to speak it?

With respect to the question of truth, a missional hermeneutic does not deny that in an important sense the gospel is always "true-for-you." There is always a concrete, particular, local sense in which the gospel addresses us. A missional hermeneutic recognizes and affirms the postmodern emphasis on the contingent, local and particular. However, the truth of the gospel can never be simply relegated to the sphere of the private, local and particular. The gospel's claim to offer good news of cosmic significance is a constant prod to Christians to reach beyond their own enclaves to address and challenge their culture and world with the gracious and hopeful claim that Jesus is Lord.

At the same time, that truth of the gospel — if indeed

it is the gospel's truth — is always spoken and interpreted in love. It is never spoken for the purpose of political control or domination but in the hope that each person and community might discover its true voice and its own distinctive experience of full humanity as the gospel takes root in fresh and diverse ways. *How* we speak is as important to our missional vocation as *what* we speak. In this sense, Newbigin (1989:222ff.) is quite right to speak of the local congregation as the hermeneutic of the gospel. It is ultimately through our lives, in all of their contingency and local particularity, that the universal claim of the gospel will find a credible voice in the midst of our fragmented and suspicious world. It is only when the announcement "Jesus is Lord" is spoken by someone who takes the posture of a servant that it can ever be heard as the gospel. It is only through the convergence of word and deed that the fragmented suspicion of our postmodern world will be able to discover a new Way that is also Truth and Life.

In this effort to speak the truth in love, Scripture itself provides us a reliable guide. It models for us a flexible hermeneutic that holds Christian faith together within the framework of the gospel yet affirms the validity and necessity of diverse expressions of Christian faith within the pluralist and conversational structure of the canon itself. May our own expressions of Christian faith be similarly grounded in the gospel and held together within the pluralist and conversational structures and practices of the worldwide church of Jesus Christ.

Notes

1. For a helpful survey of different formulations of "the gospel" in the New Testament, see Dunn (1977).

2. See, for example, C. H. Dodd's (1937) classic study. Although Dodd's study is not without its flaws, it does document how the issue of Jesus' identity and death is pervasive in early Christian preaching.

3. Numerous other summary statements could be cited, e.g., John 16:33b; Rom. 1:16; 1 Cor. 15:1–5; Phil. 2:5–11; 1 Tim. 2:5–6; Titus 3:4–7; Heb. 1:1–4; 1 Pet. 1:3; 1 John 3:8b, 5:1; Rev. 5:9–10.

4. Yet the use of the indicative "you pay taxes" in 13:6 does suggest that the Roman Christians are not already refusing to pay taxes. Paul is probably not seeking to rein in revolutionary forces but rather to provide a theological grounding for something the Roman Christians are already doing.

5. See, for example, the discussion of the phase "peace and security" in 1 Thessalonians 5:3 in Klaus Wengst (1987:76–79). Wengst argues that Paul quotes a common Roman slogan "peace and security" and that Paul goes on to expose the illusory and unsustainable character of that kind of peace, in the light of the coming judgment of God.

6. Note, for example, how the governor Felix keeps Paul in prison even though he knows that he is innocent, "since he wanted to grant the Jews a favor" (Acts 24:27).

7. Wengst (1987, 104) writes regarding the "triumphal entry," for example, "For [Luke] the entry of Jesus into Jerusalem is the

beginning of a heavenly enthronement which has nothing to do with a present manifestation of the Kingdom of God."

8. For further discussion, see Rensberger (1988:90ff.). I am indebted to Rensberger's helpful discussion at many points in my treatment of this passage.

9. The text is ambiguous as to whether Jesus or Pilate sits on the judge's bench, but both lexical and contextual clues suggest that Jesus is the one who is seated.

10. John 19:11a has at times erroneously been interpreted as indicating a divine authorization of the Roman government, but it is probably best to read this statement in a more restricted fashion, as applying to this particular incident rather than to "the state" in some general way.

References Cited

Bauckham, Richard. 1993. *The Theology of the Book of Revelation.* Cambridge: Cambridge University Press.

Bultmann, Rudolf. "Ist Voraussetzunglose Exegese Möglich?" in *Theologische Zeitschrift*, XIII (1957), 409–17. ET: "Is Exegesis without Presuppositions Possible?" In *Existence and Faith: Shorter Writings of Rudolf Bultmann.* Cleveland and New York: Meridian Books, 1960. Pp. 289–96.

Dodd, C. H. 1937. *The Apostolic Preaching and Its Development.* Chicago: Willett, Clark and Co.

Dunn, James D. G. 1977. *Unity and Diversity in the New Testament.* Philadelphia: Westminster Press.

Friedrich, Gerhard. 1965. "εὐγγελίζομαι." In *Theological Dictionary of the New Testament.* Vol. 2. Ed. G. Kittel. Grand Rapids: Eerdmans.

Gadamer, Hans-Georg. *Truth and Method.* New York: Seabury Press, 1975.

Hauerwas, Stanley, and William Willimon. 1989. *Resident Aliens: Life in the Christian Community.* Nashville: Abingdon Press.

Kelsey, David. 1975. *The Uses of Scripture in Recent Theology.* Philadelphia: Fortress Press.

MacIntyre, Alasdair. 1988. *Whose Justice? Which Rationality?* Notre Dame: University of Notre Dame Press.

Moxnes, Halvor. 1991. "Patron-Client Relations and the New Community in Luke-Acts." In *The Social World of Luke-Acts: Models for Interpretation.* Ed. Jerome H. Neyrey. Peabody, MA: Hendrickson.

Newbigin, Lesslie. 1986. *Foolishness to the Greeks.* Grand Rapids: Eerdmans.

———. 1989. *The Gospel in a Pluralist Society.* Grand Rapids: Eerdmans/Geneva: WCC Publications.

Rensberger, David. 1988. *Johannine Faith and Liberating Community.* Philadelphia: Westminster Press.

Sanneh, Lamin. 1989. *Translating the Message: The Missionary Impact on Culture.* Maryknoll, N.Y.: Orbis Books.

Thiselton, Anthony C. *The Two Horizons: New Testament Hermeneutics and Philosophical Description with Special Reference to Heidegger, Bultmann, Gadamer, and Wittgenstein.* Grand Rapids: Eerdmans and Exeter: Paternoster, 1980.

Wengst, Klaus. 1987. *Pax Romana and the Peace of Jesus Christ.* Philadelphia: Fortress Press.